The Education of Teachers

The Education of Teachers

WALTER K. BEGGS

*Dean of Teachers College
University of Nebraska*

4 | 9 8 7

The Center for Applied Research in Education, Inc.
New York

Library of Congress
Catalog Card No.: 65-10983

Printed in the United States of America

Foreword

Even in these times of educational turbulence it may well be that no other sector of the whole curriculum is in such flux as the professional education of teachers. One hopes that the result will be clear gain, but one must face the danger that it will be net loss. Much of the force behind the flux has been in the order of "sloganeering" and the promotion or defense of vested interests, and those are rarely conducive to sound problem solving. There is desperate need for calm, rational analysis and cooperative planning.

Professional education has long been held in low esteem by the "academicians," who have argued for more emphasis on academic background and less on "how to teach." More important, it has been viewed with something close to disdain by a large proportion of the teachers themselves. Most important of all—but rarely stated—is the fact that it has been ineffective in producing the very educational behavior which is its goal. There can be no question at all but that professional education has long been in need of drastic overhaul.

The energy which has finally created action has come from another direction. When the American people became disturbed about their schools, they put most of the blame on the professional educationist. That led, naturally, to questioning what he was doing as he educated their teachers. On campus, this lent support to the academicians' views. The support was bolstered by generous foundation funds. Legislatures and other control bodies moved in with impulsive and often restrictive action. Finally, the argument has moved all the way up from the local campus to the national accrediting bodies. The argument is that these bodies overcontrol teacher preparation and that their bias is on the "professional" side.

It is truly wonderful that teacher education should be taken so seriously. The "great debate" is always one of democracy's major resources; but in the crude, "either-or" thinking and in the polemics of charge and countercharge, two grave dangers arise: The great and essential intellectual contributions of the professional educationist and his allies in the social and behavioral sciences—with the tremendous strides they have made in recent years—may be underused; their further research and development may be inhibited; and the creative program improvements which have made so fine a start may only be slowed up. At the same time, a smug self-assurance may cover up the need for refined curriculum planning and improved instruction in the liberal arts sector, where every discerning educator knows that a great teacher education problem exists. It is all to the good that teachers are coming to have more background in the liberal arts; but what they need is a truly *liberal* education, and that, as Conant has pointed out, is not easy to come by in today's colleges.

Onto this scene comes Dean Walter K. Beggs of the University of Nebraska. A seasoned high school teacher and administrator, an experienced professor of education, and now the head of a great teachers college, he is, nevertheless, a long way from being a captive of the educationists' traditional views. In this volume he uses his skill as a historian to develop a long perspective. Then he delves into the heart of the issues and problems. His factual description of the key organizations and their work has not been equaled anywhere. His willingness to look with equanimity at considerations of many types is rarely matched.

There is every evidence that Dean Beggs' work comes at precisely the right moment—when the bitterness is going out of the debate and people are ready for constructive action. The great problem now is to go forward, to secure the best possible schools by developing the best possible teachers. To those pondering how to accomplish that, this book offers, not the answers, but a solid background of fact and a true perspective of the long development to the present status of teacher preparation.

FRED T. WILHELMS

Associate Secretary
National Association of
*   Secondary-School Principals*

The Education of Teachers

Walter K. Beggs

Probably no issue in American education has in modern times excited so much general interest as the proper preparation of teachers for the schools of the nation. In his volume, *The Education of Teachers,* Dr. Beggs faces squarely the controversial points of view on the subject. His treatment is soundly based on an examination of the historical development of teacher education, not only in the United States, but extending as far back as Ancient Greece. He does not attempt a state-by-state description of present practices in the preparation of teachers and in certification requirements; rather, he cites the generally accepted patterns and indicates something of the variations to be found between and among states and among institutions. It would seem, from a reading of his monograph, that much of the recent controversy about the education of teachers might have been avoided if there had been a wider understanding about both the past and the present in teacher education. Dr. Beggs's book should be required prerequisite reading for anyone who proposes to criticize present programs or to make suggestions for their improvement.

Dr. Beggs does not limit his presentation to a recounting of what has been and what is. As a summary to his findings about teacher preparation, he presents a series of constructive suggestions, projecting the kind of person needed as a teacher and the means by which such a person can best be prepared. His suggestions involve the consideration of the impact of the learning process on the pupil as the central concern in evaluating plans for teacher education. He bases his ideas on an analysis of the situation in contemporary society and the directions in which changes are taking place.

Dr. Beggs is concerned in this volume with the classroom teacher at the elementary and secondary levels, and chiefly with what is known as preservice education. Although he refers to the general requirement that, under modern standards, a teacher is expected to continue to make additional preparation for some years after first entering teaching, he does not treat in detail the nature of that sort of program. He does not discuss the preparation of kinds of school personnel other than the classroom teacher, or the kinds of personnel needed at educational levels other than the elementary school or the high school. Among other volumes in the Library of Education, that have parallel treatment of the preparation of other kinds of educational personnel, may be mentioned: *In-Service Education for Teachers,* by Moffitt; *The Supervisor,* by McKean and Mills; *The School Counselor,* by Roeber; *The School Psychologist,* by Eiserer; and *The College President,* by Prator.

JOHN DALE RUSSELL
Content Editor

Contents

ix

CHAPTER I

Historical Antecedents

Teaching no longer consists merely of passing on the simple skills, customs, rituals, and art forms of the family or tribe; it has developed into the interrelated, sequential, and complex pattern that confronts the highly specialized professionals of the present time. A long and involved narrative would be necessary to trace the whole development,[1] but this type of reporting is not the intention of the present treatise. Any current situation, however, is meaningful only when viewed in relation to its historical antecedents, so the background of the modern scene will be sketched as it relates to teaching and especially to teacher education.

In a simple social structure such as the family or tribe, practically all basic instruction is done by parents. They teach their offspring by showing them how to do things or by encouraging their own movements to be emulated as a form of play. The process is direct and unsophisticated. Even in the most primitive of tribes, however, rituals and customs develop, and often these become highly formalized. When this happens, the responsibility for passing on the institutionalized tribal heritage is generally assigned to prestige members of the community, such as elders or priests. A sort of crude methodology is developed, and hence the embryo ingredients of formalized instruction and specialized teaching are present.[2]

Historically, as the tribes developed more intricate patterns and merged into fairly elaborate social units, more and more formalization of processes appeared. The simple skills and rituals were ver-

---

[1] Unfortunately, no comprehensive coverage of the evolution of teacher education has ever been written, except as it appears in general treatments of the educational or cultural development of civilization. For this type of reference, see Freeman R. Butts, *A Cultural History of Education* (New York: McGraw-Hill Book Company, 1947). See also James Mulhern, *A History of Education,* 2nd ed. (New York: The Ronald Press Company, 1959).

[2] Frederick Eby and Charles Flinn Arrowood, *History and Philosophy of Education* (Englewood Cliffs, N.J.: Prentice-Hall, Inc., 1940), Chap. I. For more comprehensive coverage, see Ruth Benedict, *Patterns of Culture* (Boston: Houghton Mifflin Company, 1943).

balized for broader communication. Scattered bits of knowledge
were joined into related patterns, symbols were introduced, systems
were developed, and knowledge was eventually categorized into
sophisticated disciplines. Knowledge was first symbolized and organized, then formalized, and finally related into interlocking systems.[3]

Each step had its implications for teachers. The developments in
teacher education directly followed the routes taken by the human
family in developing its social orders from the very simple to the
very complex.

The Teacher in Antiquity

By the year 500 B.C., a number of quite highly developed societies
had emerged. Most of them had produced the elements of an educational system and some formal schools. Curricular patterns can be
identified, and the purposes of education were fairly well delineated.
In most instances, however, teaching was still the responsibility of
the priesthood, or elders, or special eminences whose prestige in
other matters won them the role of teaching. In short, teaching as a
separate professional practice had not as yet put in an appearance.

The Sophists.   The first brief appearance of anything remotely
resembling a professional teacher came when a band of itinerants
called Sophists emerged in Athens between 500 and 400 B.C.[4] In a
way, they represented a school of philosophy expressed by the most
distinguished of their number, Protagoras, who believed that man
is the measure of all things and that truth is what each person perceives or thinks it to be. The Sophists attacked the rigidity and narrowness of education and introduced a liberal intellectualism into
their teaching. Mulhern maintains that they were the first exponents
of true liberal education.[5] Actually, many of them were pseudo
scholars, and the worst were little more than educational charlatans.
They did, however, experiment with organizing knowledge so that
it could be better taught, and, especially, they taught with a specific
purpose. Apparently they considered teaching a specialized skill un-

---

[3] Eby and Arrowood, *op. cit.,* pp. 53–70.
[4] These dates are not intended to be definitive, but rather to establish the time
when the Sophists were most active. Protagoras, for example, was born in 486 B.C.
[5] Mulhern, *op. cit.,* p. 152.

related to the subject matter under consideration. Hence they studied the structure of language and taught it as a tool to be used in self-expression, if not self-aggrandizement. Rhetoric was their favorite subject, although they would teach anything for which they were paid. Logic was another of their specialties, although they were accused of using logic as a method of winning debates rather than as a means of establishing truth. Doubtless they deserved some of the contempt in which they were held by their better known contemporaries. Nevertheless, their brief appearance in the spotlight of history was the first instance in which teaching appears as an indigenous function in the fabric of society, capable of establishing a special relationship with learners both individually and in groups.[6]

Ancient patterns of teaching. It is probably unfortunate that the Sophists were not able to establish their particular pattern of teaching more firmly than they did, but apparently so many of them were of low scholastic caliber that their unique approach to instruction tended to become equated with mediocrity. In any event, whatever they contributed was greatly overshadowed by some of their illustrious contemporaries.

Socrates was possibly the most famous of the ancient teachers, although he was more philosopher than teacher. His great thesis was built around the power of reason: that society endures and maintains stability only as all men seek truth, think rationally, and expand their knowledge and wisdom. He sought to establish these values in his students, and he developed a procedure in his teaching which has come to be known as the Socratic Method. He would elicit the reactions of his students and then by clever questioning lead them to the conclusion that their opinions were in error, and by further questioning stimulate them to inquire more deeply into the subject. This process of inducing a learner to take a position, then by a kind of intellectual flanking movement force him to defend and strengthen his stand or move to a better posture, is an excellent design for fostering mental growth. It does presuppose, however, a very high intellectual maturity for the teacher and a relatively broad development on the part of the student.[7]

Plato, as contrasted to Socrates, sought the perfect society in order

---

[6] For an extensive study of the Sophists, see Mario Untersteiner, *The Sophists* (New York: New York Philosophical Library, 1934).

[7] Eby and Arrowood, *op. cit.*, p. 321*ff*.

and discipline, and he attempted to define man's place in it. Education, he maintained, is a process of moral training, and since virtue is knowledge, and knowledge can be taught, then virtue can be taught. The first objective of education is state unity, followed by civic efficiency, esthetic sensibility, harmonizing of body, mind, and environment, and finally living together in harmony. All knowledge, being innate, is fixed and unchangeable. Hence, teaching is a process of promulgating the ideal or, as it would be termed today, instructing the learner in discerning right from wrong. Plato's philosphy permeated educational thinking until modern times, and it is still the major influence in many quarters.[8]

To Aristotle, education was a function of the state, and its objective was to produce happiness through the development of (1) health, (2) fame and honor as a citizen, (3) wise use of leisure, (4) good moral character, and (5) the intellectual faculties. As the basis and preparation for advanced learning, his methods were demonstration, induction, and, particularly, direct experience.[9]

Socrates, Plato, and Aristotle have probably exerted a more profound influence on subsequent generations of scholars than they did on their own society. Be that as it may, granting each his peculiar philosophical frame of reference, together they symbolize a type of teaching that has come to be looked upon as characteristic of the true intellectual as a mentor. A man of great mental gifts contemplates the physical and societal environment around him. He perceives certain relationships. From the relationships he proposes theories which he submits to the most severe tests of logic that he, or the contemporaries he respects, can devise. When his theories have stood the tests, he weaves a general philosophy from them which he constantly refines by repeating the procedure. Then he propounds his philosophy to students, explains the theories on which it is based, and attempts to induce an emulation of his intellectual processes, if not an acceptance of his philosophy.

In theory, at least, each of the disciples of the eminent scholar will evolve his own constellation of students, and the leaven of great learning spreads.[10] In practical application, however, only a small

---

[8] Mulhern, *op. cit.*, p. 156*ff*.

[9] *Ibid.*, p. 166*ff*.

[10] This actually was the case with the three Grecian philosophies we have described here. Plato was a student of Socrates and, in turn, taught Aristotle.

fraction of the human family seems capable of this level of intellectual activity, or will exert the quality of mental discipline necessary to indulge in it. It is interesting to note that Socrates, Plato, and Aristotle accepted as axiomatic that the great masses of people were equipped to assimilate only rudimentary instruction, which the three considered vulgar and relatively unimportant. In this category were the manual skills necessary to routine work or the higher skills of the artisan, along with the elementary mental exercises necessary for day by day existence. Hence, most of the people in Grecian society were outside the pale of formal schooling and were relegated to apprenticeship or whatever informal agencies were available to them for learning experiences.

The structure of the ancient cultures gradually disintegrated and merged into new and different sociopolitical configurations. The forces at work to cause their decline were many and quite complex. Turner, in *Great Cultural Traditions,* ascribed their fall (in part at least) to the inability of their leadership to bridge the gap between what he called the high and low cultural traditions. In other words, the extremes represented on the continuum of human ability tend to drift apart. They cease to gain inspiration from each other and thus lose all communication. Each eventually begins to hate and despise the values held by the other. If there is no middle superstructure to serve as a buttress and a channel of communication between the extremes, the culture topples into the void separating them.[11]

A middle structure or social stratum probably could not have existed for long in the political and social climate of the ancient and classical cultures. This is a moot point, because a merchant class did develop in both Greece and Rome as well as in some other civilizations, but it apparently never was rooted very deeply; and no one, even the greatest of the philosophers, seemed able to imagine—much less invent—a structure with free and unsanctioned interclass mobility.[12]

Although the great minds of the ancient world left an indelible mark on the educational adventures of civilization, they failed to sup-

---

11 Ralph E. Turner, *The Great Cultural Traditions,* 2 Vols. (New York: McGraw-Hill Book Company, 1941). This is the author's interpretation of Turner and may be somewhat oversimplified, but it is in general keeping with Turner's thesis.

12 John Geise, *Man and the Western World* (New York: Harcourt, Brace & World, Inc., 1940), pp. 67–69, 82–85, 261–63.

ply the principle catalyst for blending the components of Western culture. This ingredient was supplied through the teaching and the philosophy of Jesus of Nazareth. There is nothing particularly remarkable to be noted about his methods, but no historian denies the power of his simple and direct use of conversation, proverbs, and parables in raising the aspirations and hopes of his followers and in lifting them to a higher plane of thought and deed. Even greater than the power of his teaching has been the strength of the ethos he propounded. By it, man has significance quite apart from any relation to his material or social environment. He is sacred in the sight of God, and thus his worth transcends his ancestry, his peculiar abilities, his station in life, or at any given moment what he has done with his talents or his life. Apart from its ecclesiastical concepts, and doctrinaire interpretations the Hebraic Christian Ethic has exerted the most profound influence of any element in man's progressive experience.[13]

The Changing Cultural Scene

Space does not permit more than a brief outline of the interlocking complex of elements involved in shaping the course of Western civilization. As the succeeding generations grew away from their ancient heritage, a number of major forces seem to be involved in shaping the course of events.

Forces that brought cultural change. The forces that are included here are not listed necessarily in order of significance, nor are they intended to be all inclusive. Six are suggested as illustrative of the complex elements that elevated man considerably in his quest for a better life: (1) the impact of the Hebraic Christian Ethic; (2) the invention of paper and printing; (3) the revival of learning; (4) the advent of scientific inquiry; (5) the industrial revolution; and (6) the rise of capitalism.[14]

Many other factors were involved also—factors which were instrumental in moving society from the relative provincial and parochial communities which characterized the ancient and medieval cultures, through a transition period to the highly complex, inter-

---

[13] *Ibid.*, pp. 295–96, 735–36.
[14] For more comprehensive coverage see Geise, *op. cit.*, Chaps. 18, 19, 20, and 21.

related dynamic of modern Western civilization. To argue whether mankind is better as a result is not the purpose of this discussion. Instead, the intent is to show that the forces had a profound effect on the way men lived, on the nature of their institutions, and particularly on the pattern of the educational structures that were developed.

Changes that impinged on educational development. As capitalism, the industrial revolution, the inroads of scientific inquiry, and the resurgence of interest in learning of all kinds gradually altered the structure of Western society, formal education came to be recognized as one of the basic ingredients necessary to the successful operation of the complicated cultural machinery. The systems of schools and colleges that were developed furthered and accelerated the changes. Several of these were strategic and may be listed briefly to round out the description of the broad foundations on which modern education rests.

1. The gradual advent of social mobility.
2. The emergence of a cultural mean—the middle class.
3. The growing consciousness of diverse human needs.
4. The emergence of education as a social tool.
5. The tendency for education to become universal.[15]

The impact of changes so vast, with the attendant reconsideration of the kind of schools necessary in the emerging new social structure, was paralleled with new interest in the process of training teachers for the schools.

The Evolution of Teacher Education
in the American System

It is generally held that the process listed as item five above has been developed further in the United States than anywhere else in the world. Without reference to quality of product or excellence of process, this is probably true. It is also true that the development in the United States has followed a route different from that in other countries.

Cultural commitments of the United States. As the nation has evolved, certain commitments have been made to the way in which

---

[15] *Idem.*

the society shall develop and be operated.[16] These are naturally kaleidoscopic, and their application keeps shifting and changing with the different pressures that are encountered. Beginning with the Declaration of Independence and the Constitution, and following through the many facets of application and interpretation, the American people have committed themselves to developing and maintaining a society in which the individual can grow to his fullest capacity, in which opportunity is unlimited and unimpeded, in which the contributions of all levels and types of ability are welcomed and encouraged, and in which worth is evaluated according to the individual's capacity and contribution. Although the nation, in many instances, has fallen far short of achieving these ideals, it is remarkable that they are still basically the target for social and cultural achievement.

The society has also committed itself to provide agencies and institutions to assist in meeting its objectives. Among these are a wide variety of agencies and institutions of an ameliorative and correctional nature, both private and public, and a school system that is purposefully universal, free, compulsory, and comprehensive.

Implications of the commitments for education. When schools accept the children of the total range of the population, when attendance is compulsory, and especially when comprehensiveness in program is attempted, careful attention to common and individual needs is implied. This, in turn, results in varied curriculums, flexibility in offerings and approach, and a sensitivity to cultural needs, especially to cultural change. An educational effort of such magnitude requires tremendous resources, a vast structural organization, and an equally large teaching, administrative, and servicing staff.

In the United States, by Constitutional implication the basic responsibility for education belongs to the states. These have delegated some of the policy-making prerogatives to various governmental subunits, such as counties, cities, and townships; but usually the prerogatives have been delegated to chartered school districts, which may or may not be coterminous with any of the above-named units. In general, the rationale has been that policy for the day by day control and operation of the schools is better left to the locality which provides the students, is most immediately affected, and pro-

---

[16] James Truslow Adams, *The Epic of America* (Boston: Little, Brown & Co., 1933), Chaps. IV, VI, and X. See also E. P. Cubberley, *Public Education in the United States* (New York: Houghton Mifflin Company, 1934), Chaps. V–IX.

vides a large part of the financial support either directly or indirectly. This whole process operates under an over-all framework of general state policy stipulated in the state constitution and statutes.

The peculiar approach to building an educational structure in the United States has led to an equally distinctive pattern in the evolution of teacher education.

The normal-school movement. The school system of this country was in reality built community by community. The states have been held responsible, but in the early years of national development state efforts were at best minimal. At present there is much more concentration of policy making and control at the state level, and a growing interest at the national level, both in governmental and non-governmental agencies. Even so the imprint of locality, the intense local interest, and the sensitivity to local and regional needs gave the schools their peculiar "grass roots" complexion.

So it was in the development of teacher education. It is not known exactly when consensus was reached that, if the schools were to have a supply of reasonably well-prepared teachers, special localized institutions for their education would have to be developed. The first state normal school (for teacher preparation) was opened at Lexington, Massachusetts, in July of 1839.[17] For some years, educators in the United States had been observing and studying educational practices in Europe. In Germany and France they discovered that teachers were trained in special and separate institutions. The idea gained acceptance in most of the New England states and spread westward. The early normal schools certainly left much to be desired. They were little more than of secondary grade. They were generally held in contempt by the colleges. They were opposed by the academies, a number of which offered their own short courses for teachers. Opponents of the public schools feared that the normal schools might be the instrument by which the movement for public education would gain the momentum it needed.

Except in Massachusetts, most of the early normal schools died out for a time. Teachers for the common schools, if trained at all, had to depend on the academies. Teachers in the academies were indifferent to special training for themselves or their colleagues. The colleges were intent on other matters. If any thought was given

---

[17] Cubberley, *op. cit.*, p. 380.

to teacher education at all, it was with disdain; hence, the normal school movement languished and almost expired.

Other forces, however, were at work in the society. The people wanted schools, and by 1890 the great battles for public education were resolved, and the cultural commitments for free, universal, and comprehensive schools had been established. After the Civil War the industrialization of the nation progressed rapidly, the need for literacy was great, and the demand for people educated beyond the literacy level was growing sharply. A comparable market for teachers in the common schools was developing, particularly in the middle West. It was desired that these teachers have some concept of the process of teaching and some degree of empathy for the children of "ordinary people." The normal schools appeared to be the answer.

These little institutions were crude. They made no effort to be scholarly or even limitedly academic. They had a single purpose—to produce teachers in quantity—and this they proceeded to do. In the process they developed a sort of *modus operandi:* (1) Make sure that the prospective teacher knows the fundamentals of what he proposes to teach, at least a little above the level of mastery he expects of his students. (2) Give him a little training in how to organize the subject matter and to plan his presentation. (3) Teach him a few formulas for managing a classroom situation and controlling students. (4) Wherever possible, let him observe an experienced teacher in operation. (5) Have him teach under supervision for a time to get the actual feel of the situation and to gain the advantage of a more or less professional critique of his performance.

The last two functions were not always possible at the start, but gradually they became an integral part of the normal-school program, along with two other areas—an embryonic knowledge and acqaintance with how learning takes place in the growth of a human being, and a similarly embryonic knowledge of society and education's place in it. This general format is still the skeletal structure for programs of teacher preparation; and, with variations in emphasis, it will probably remain so.[18]

Jessie Pangburn has noted a number of factors which from 1890 to 1930 conditioned the evolution of the normal schools from secondary grade institutions, training only elementary teachers, to the

---

[18] See Chap. II.

single-purpose teachers college which included prospective high school teachers among its enrollees.[19] Among the factors involved, she lists: (1) the local control of education, (2) the rising qualifications of teachers, (3) the centralization of administrative authority, (4) expansion of the school system, (5) increased quality in the educational effort, (6) the rapid development of the high school, and (7) the impact of accrediting associations.

In addition, an organized approach to the study of teacher education, which had its inception in Europe, was beginning to have an impact. The writings of Rousseau, Pestalozzi, Herbart, and others were being carefully studied. In the United States, Mann and Barnard, G. Stanley Hall, Henry James, and John Dewey, among others, were establishing the teacher as a professional of considerable stature, and his education as a process requiring much more than elementary knowledge and a few exercises in practicum.

Meanwhile, the nation was growing out of its frontier experiences and was becoming stabilized as a world power. After the European conflict of 1914–1918, the high schools and colleges graduated an increasing number of students; and these, in turn, demanded more and better education for their children. First, the high school diploma and, later, the college degree became status symbols. The academic community—which first ignored, then viewed with contempt, and finally grudgingly accepted teacher education as a channel of college work—began to reassert its influence for quality all along the educational route.

Thus, the twentieth century has been a period in which there was a remarkable rise in the quality of teacher education programs. First, a floor of general liberal education was placed under the preparation program. Second, the development of postgraduate work in specialization added strength. Finally, a much more careful screening, selection, and retention of candidates was established for the training and certification of teachers.

In summary, teacher education in the United States reflects a blending of the social and educational heritage of Western civilization, along with the peculiar cultural commitments of the people of

---

[19] Jessie M. Pangburn, *The Evolution of the American Teachers College* (New York: Bureau of Publications, Teachers College, Columbia University, 1932), pp. 2–12.

the United States. Currently, the whole structure, approach, and direction of teacher education is in a state of flux. From a beginning which was largely local and fragmented, it has developed to the point where it is a national issue of considerable significance.

CHAPTER II

The Current Situation—
Institutions, Programs, Students

In Chapter I it was noted that during the last decades of the nineteenth century, most of the colleges had begun teacher education, and that schools and colleges of education emerged as an integral part of multipurpose universities. This latter phase has been almost entirely a twentieth-century development.[1]

Teacher education is now exclusively a college function. If any high school departments of normal training still remain, they are destined to disappear rapidly. However, the evolution in the organization, programs, and general processes involved in the education of teachers continues. In this chapter the purpose is to describe the institutions as they now exist, to define their programs, to give a resumé of the curricular content, and to look briefly at the quality of students engaged in seeking certification for teaching.

Types of Institutions

Almost every college or university in the United States is engaged in some form of teacher education. A few disclaim any interest. Yale, for example, has discontinued its school of education, as have some highly specialized institutions, such as the Massachusetts Institute of Technology and the California Institute of Technology; but these are a very small minority.[2]

The colleges and universities that maintain some type of program of teacher education can be divided roughly into four categories: (1) the teachers colleges, (2) four-year liberal arts colleges, (3) multipurpose universities, and (4) graduate schools of education.

---

[1] This implies only that the acceleration came in the twentieth century. Many colleges had begun to train teachers, and some had established departments or schools of education before 1900.

[2] Yale maintains a Master of Arts in Teaching programs for Liberal Arts, and a relationship with the New Haven Teachers College to service undergraduates in professional education.

The single-purpose teachers college. The teachers college as it originally developed was a direct descendant of the normal school, but the original version is now almost as obsolete as its parent. Even the name "Teachers College" is being replaced by "State College" or sometimes by "State College of Education." Very few of these institutions still confine themselves exclusively to teacher education curriculums.. Many have added programs leading to the Bachelor of Arts degree. Graduate work for the Master of Education or Master of Arts degrees is not unusual, and a few of the larger institutions are attempting doctoral degrees.

The point at which a teachers college becomes another type of institution is hard to determine. A case in point is Northern Illinois University.[3] It was chartered in 1895 as the Northern Illinois State Normal School with a two-year curriculum. In 1921 the program was extended to four years and the Bachelor of Education Degree was authorized. In 1943 the degree designation was changed to Bachelor of Science in Education, and in 1951 graduate work leading to the Master of Science in Education was added. The institution became Northern Illinois State College in 1955, and curriculums leading to the degrees of Bachelor of Arts and Bachelor of Science were authorized. Two years later, in 1957, the name was again changed to Northern Illinois University, and since that time the institution has been reorganized into colleges and doctoral degrees have been approved.

In spite of this sequence of changes, a curious fact remains: "Although provision for other interests is made, teacher education continues to be the major function of Northern Illinois University," and teacher education claims about 75 per cent of the students. As the institution grows in enrollment and a university atmosphere in the truest sense begins to pervade the campus, this emphasis will obviously soften and the percentage of students in the teaching curriculum will decline.

The peculiar emphasis in the program of a college is of more significance than the ratio of students in the various specialties. Regardless of size, an institution still remains a teachers college if the major concern of the curriculum is directed toward the specialized needs of students who are preparing to teach. This does not mean

---

[3] Faculty Self-Study Report, Northern Illinois University, 1963. (mimeographed).

that the bulk of the work is confined to courses in methods and pedagogy. Contrary to a popular misconception, roughly four fifths of the most modern programs in teacher education is devoted to the subject disciplines and to general education.[4] In the single-purpose teachers colleges somewhat more time may be spent on pedagogical matters, but the difference is in emphasis, not in the quantity or quality of subject matter. In an institution with the teachers-college orientation, a bias is discernible always toward what the student is going to do with what he learns. Subject-matter courses will be taught with the idea that the students will in turn reteach the material, or at least a part of it, to other learners on a lower level. Hence, while mastery of the subject is generally expected and intellectual maturity encouraged, the objective is not necessarily to produce a student who is a research specialist or a highly creative scholar. It is assumed that the future teacher will need to know the structure of the discipline because he will have to organize it into teachable units. He must be able to translate it into various apperception levels so that it will be meaningful to learners less intellectually mature than himself. He must necessarily be concerned with the wide divergence in mentality of a given age group. The teacher must be concerned with how a learner can be motivated to become interested in the material, how he will react to it, and how he may use it in his personal pattern of growth and development.

The faculty of the so-called single-purpose teachers college respects the needs of prospective teachers and pays particular attention to them.[5] In this type of institution the faculty is not generally research oriented, nor is it necessarily expected to do much research; it is neither encouraged nor discouraged. Teaching, however (hopefully, master teaching), is expected, encouraged, and rewarded as the highest level on the scale of values.[6]

At some point in the transition from single to multipurpose organization, the emphasis on teaching shifts from being regarded as the major contribution of the institution's faculty to being one of several functions, perhaps even one of secondary importance. Research and production, writing, and scholarly pursuits generally become the

---

[4] This figure refers to secondary majors. Students in Elementary Education will have more professional work.

[5] Faculty Self-Study Report, Colorado State College, Greeley, Colorado, 1961, pp. 7–8 (mimeographed).

[6] *Ibid.*, p. 6.

principal activities, and teaching is relegated to a parallel, if not a less desirable, expenditure of effort.

The difference between these factors is in emphasis and is not readily visible. It is, in fact, an institutionalized phenomenon existing in the community of higher education that almost has to be "lived with" to be comprehended. It bears examination in any discussion of teacher education because so many of the former teachers colleges are growing rapidly and experiencing the problems of transition. Moreover, the leadership in teacher education appears to be shifting away from the one-time single-purpose colleges to the multipurposé universities. The final impact of this shift is not completely apparent as yet, but some major changes are almost inevitable.[7]

The four-year liberal arts college.   During the nineteenth century and the first two decades of the twentieth century, hundreds of liberal arts colleges sprang up over the United States.[8] In the main they were denominationally related and religiously oriented. Their avowed purpose originally was to provide a liberal education in a "Christian environment." Almost always at their inception, they were ecclesiastical in their intent, centering on the promulgation of the particular doctrine of the denomination involved. Strong courses in Bible and theology were prominent features of their programs for both preministerial training and for general education for all students. The growth and development pattern has varied from institution to institution. Some have become large multipurpose universities. Others have experienced growth, but they have retained at least a modicum of their original characteristics. Almost universally, the scope of their programs has been broadened to include preprofessional curriculums and, in many instances, vocational or professional courses of varying kinds. In the main, however, these colleges claimed (and still claim) to be nonvocational in orientation. Although they frankly admit that their graduates must somehow make a living, specialization is not their forte, but rather a broad, general, and liberal education. Their aim is to produce graduates "that exhibit the marks of an educated human being."

---

[7] See page 19 this chapter.

[8] No comprehensive treatment of this movement is available. However, it is available in fragments from a number of publications, such as Frank E. Weyer, *Presbyterian Colleges and Academies in Nebraska* (Hastings, Nebr.: Hastings College, 1940).

There is no documented record available to indicate when, or how, or under what circumstances teacher education became a part of the program of the liberal arts colleges.[9] During the earlier years of their development, any of their students who wished could teach on the strength of their baccalaureate degrees, or even on the basis of a few hours of college work. As the states began to be more explicit in certification requirements, the colleges added the courses and faculty necessary to meet the demands of the certification laws. Hence, teachers of pedagogy or education, and classes in methods, tests and measurements, child psychology, and history of education began to appear in the liberal arts college. Then a normal course, or teachers curriculum, was organized. Finally, a discrete pattern for teacher education emerged, and in most instances a department of education was created.[10]

The teacher output of the liberal arts colleges has been large, and their graduates have made an important contribution to education in the United States.[11] Teacher education, however, has not received emphasis as a major function of the institution. It has been an addendum, a pattern to protect the interest of those students who wish to teach and who, to do so, must meet specific requirements.

Although variations in emphasis exist from place to place, there is a certain climate about the four-year liberal arts colleges as contrasted to the teachers colleges and the larger universities. Balanced liberal education—as opposed to specialization, general study, and appreciation of the scholarly disciplines—seems to be the major characteristic of their programs. The faculties are expected to exemplify "great teaching." An inspirational classroom performance is considered the *sine qua non* of high quality. Superior scholarship is greatly admired and presumably rewarded, but the great emphasis on research that is apparent in the universities does not hold the same degree of importance here. In fact, some liberal arts colleges tend to discourage research because they believe it distracts from teaching.

The multiple-purpose university. The multipurpose university

---

[9] Except as the pattern is indicated in the college catalogs over the years.

[10] Weyer, *op. cit.*, pp. 146–71.

[11] For example, of the total graduates of Tarkio College, Tarkio, Missouri, more than 50 per cent entered teaching between 1900 and 1960. Material in author's files from a survey of this college in March 1960.

in the United States has many antecedents. Some single-purpose teachers colleges have become, or are attempting to become, multi-purpose institutions. Similarly, a one-time liberal arts college may have grown, added functions, organized into schools or colleges, and emerged as a multipurpose institution. Most of the Morrill Act colleges of agriculture and mechanical arts have now become multi-purpose universities. Whatever its antecedents, an institution which serves many purposes, is organized into a number of schools or colleges under a single administration, and has added postbaccalaureate and graduate professional college degrees may qualify in this category.

Universities exhibit a wide range in size, organization, and quality. They may have as few as 1000 or as many as 30,000 or more students on a single campus.[12] They exhibit many types of control—from the private university with a board of trustees which is completely responsible for the policies of the institution, to the public institutions which are responsible to some unit of government. A few state universities, such as in Minnesota, are constitutionally created and enjoy a marked degree of independence. Responsibility for policy making in the publicly controlled universities is almost universally vested in a lay governing board, which is either chosen in a general election or appointed by the governor or the chief executive of the branch of government involved. Some states maintain systems of higher education. California, for example, has three organized levels: the university, the state colleges, and the junior colleges. The State University of New York is a multicampus arrangement operating under a state Board of Trustees.[13]

Admission practices in state universities vary almost as much as the organizational structure. Some will accept any student who has graduated from an accredited high school. By contrast, the University of California accepts as freshmen only the upper 12½ per cent of high school graduates. Most of the private institutions maintain competitive and rather strict admissions policies.[14]

---

[12] This is a general range and refers to no particular institution.
[13] For California, see University of California, General Catalog, Vol. 57, No. 11, pp. 9–10, July, 1963; for New York, see Henry M. Brickel, *Organizing New York State for Educational Change* (New York: State Education Department, 1961).
[14] Harvard Catalog.

Teacher education, with a few exceptions, is now an integral part of the program of the multipurpose universities. In most cases, the preparation of teachers is considered important enough to be vested in a college, school, or division, in which the faculty has autonomous or at least semiautonomous control over entrance policies, curriculum construction, graduation, and placement.

There is some conviction that the most important development in teacher education in the twentieth century has been the large universities' acceptance of major responsibility in this area. The preparation of teachers is thus placed in an environment where the scholarly disciplines have their greatest strength and where the major resources of higher education currently exist. Moreover, it is possible in the university to provide close articulation between graduate and undergraduate programs, as well as to draw upon the research strength of cognate and related areas.

Whether or not the claimed advantages can be documented, the paramount issues and problems involved in the preparation of teachers are brought into sharp focus in a multiple-purpose university. The school or college of education must fit its program into the over-all policies of the institution. It must compete for resources with the powerful professional colleges, such as those of law, medicine, dentistry, and engineering. Most critical of all, it must evolve a working arrangement with the academic division or divisions of the university, since almost all the work in general education and academic specialization will be taken in these divisions. Indeed, one of the most serious points of contention between the education and academic faculties centers in the question: to which unit does teacher education belong? To the layman, this argument appears academic and pointless, and were it not for the fact that the two groups are rooted in separate heritages, the differences would be pedantic, if not silly. Actually, they represent two ends of a continuum. The academician is concerned with a discipline, an organized body of knowledge. He is jealous of its integrity; he seeks to understand its origin, its development, and its complexity. He is interested in the nuances and overtones that radiate from it, and he desires to push back the frontiers of the area, to discover new knowledge, or to refine what is already known. Teaching is a related but secondary function, and it is pursued to one end—the intellectual development of the learner.[15]

By contrast, the so-called professional in teacher education places the act of teaching at the top of the value scale, or at least on a par with scholarship. Almost as important is his concern with the function of the school in the American social order. The interest in how a human being grows from a protoplasmic embryo into a rational adult is coupled with the role of the formal agency in the culture—the school—which has been established to help nurture this process. The school is viewed as an enterprise that brings the learner into an environment specifically and formally designated to help him grow. The teacher provides the most important part of the environment, since he directs the most significant part of the process—the acquisition of knowledge and the skills basic to the growth pattern. Subject matter is viewed as an indispensable base for the whole operation, but the major goal is the growth of the learner. Hence, the professional in teacher education looks at once to the agency (the school), seeks to understand its function within the social order, seeks ways to improve it, and, most important, seeks to understand and to improve the role of the teacher within the agency.[16]

Oddly enough, the proponent at each end of the continuum sincerely feels that if his position is adequately stressed, the other will be covered as a matter of course. On the one hand, it is argued that if the student in teacher education becomes a great scholar, he can quickly master the day-by-day logistics of teaching. On the other hand, it is contended that if the student becomes firmly committed to the concept of human growth and the teaching role involved therein, he will be motivated at least to become an adequate scholar.

When two groups approaching the same task from different frames of reference are a part of the same university faculty, conflicts and tensions will surely develop, especially if the extremes are in control. If the academic faculty insists that the whole of teacher education lies in producing a scholar in the discipline and that nothing is gained from "education courses," and if the education faculty is equally adamant that mastery of a discipline is only a part of the

---

15 Nevitt Sanford, ed., *The American College* (New York: John Wiley & Sons, 1962), Chaps. III, VII, IX.

16 Donald P. Cottrell, ed., *Teacher Education for a Free People* (Oneonta, N.Y.: American Association of Colleges for Teacher Education, 1956). See Chaps. I and XI.

process and that the practicum involved in the teaching act is equally or more important, then the conflict may be indeed irreconcilable.

Fortunately, a more temperate approach to the conflict is being developed, due perhaps to the fact that both faculties have to live together in some degree of harmony on the same campus. In part, this is the result of some administrative reorganization, but it is mostly achieved through a concerted effort around the conference table to reach a compromise, if not complete understanding. The dimensions of the effort and the structure that will emerge are not as yet apparent, but the general climate of the moment is one of "give and take." The education faculties are becoming better oriented to the value structure of the academic community. The academic faculties in their turn are tending to reappraise their concept of elementary and secondary teaching, and to consider some of the problems involved in the nation's gigantic educational enterprise.

Graduate schools of education.   One of the organizational patterns that has been developed to solve, at least partially, some of the problems involved is now found in a few universities. This is the graduate school of education.[17] In these situations the professional part of teacher education is completely eliminated at the undergraduate level. The student completes his work for the baccalaureate degree as a liberal arts candidate and then specializes in professional preparation during a year or more of graduate work. This approach has both strong supporters and critics. It does, however, eliminate (or soften) some of the conflict. Once the student has completed his undergraduate work, he can concentrate on the process of becoming a teacher. He can specialize in the professional aspects of his chosen work, and he can go deeper into the area of concentration in which he proposes to teach.

Administratively, there are some pronounced advantages in this type of organization. There are fewer scheduling conflicts; the student's work can be concentrated into larger blocks of time; and he can be placed into off-campus laboratory situations with much more ease. The graduate school also provides the status advantage of placing the professional preparation of the teacher at the postbaccalau-

---

[17] Not to be confused with graduate programs in education as offered in universities which maintain standard undergraduate programs in education.

reate level, along with the major professions of law, medicine, dentistry, and some others.

Unfortunately, there are disadvantages too. In the first place, if the practice were to be universally adopted, it would force the four-year single-purpose institutions and liberal arts colleges either to add graduate work or to drop their programs of teacher education entirely. To add a fifth year to the preparation postpones the time when a young person who proposes to teach can begin to earn a livelihood and recover a part of the cost of his education. Although this is what happens in certain other professions, the earning potential is greater in most of these than in teaching. The peculiar practice of progressively upgrading teaching certificates when the teacher obtains additional education makes the first few years of experience in teaching a virtual internship.

Regardless of the arguments pro or con, the trend in the organization of teacher education may be moving in the direction of the graduate school program.

Levels and Scope of Preparation

The American school system is a complex enterprise. Basically, it is divided into three levels: the elementary school, the junior high school, and the senior high school. Each level has its own characteristics and the organization will vary accordingly.

The elementary school. Generally speaking, the elementary school is still graded; that is, children of a given age will be grouped together in the kindergarten, the first grade, and so on up through the sixth grade. Each grade is assigned to a room, or rooms, depending on the size of the school. The children will usually stay in this room throughout the school day, and most of the instruction will be given by one teacher. In short, the elementary teacher will be responsible for the same group of students for one school year and will teach all subject matter and skills required at the age-level involved, which may include reading, arithmetic, writing, spelling, English, social studies, science, or any combination of these. Music, art, and physical education are sometimes included, although, wherever possible, such subjects are generally handled by special teachers. The elementary teacher must be a generalist in subject matter and a specialist in the psychological characteristics of the age-group to be taught. Hence, a student in training may wish to concentrate on early childhood, ages five through eight, or on the upper grades, ages eight through eleven.[18]

There are a number of specialized areas that require specific preparation. These include music, art, physical education, and industrial arts. In addition, it is a growing practice in the larger school systems to employ a general director of the elementary curriculum, along with supervisory coördinators for some of, if not all, the subject areas, such as the language arts, social studies, mathematics, or science. As a result, the training colleges must gear their programs to provide preparation, not only for the general grade teacher, but for the various specializations and the administrative personnel that are required by the schools.

The junior high school. The junior high school is a peculiar American innovation designed to provide a transition between the elementary grades and the high school. As such, it exhibits some of the characteristics of both, and it presumably guides the learner through the beginning adolescent period, roughly ages 12 to 14. Some polishing of the fundamental learning skills is still necessary, but more and more the pupil begins to think and learn independently under guidance. The junior high school curriculum has been developed to meet the needs of youth in this age group.[19]

The junior high school is usually administered more like a secondary than an elementary school, and it is largely departmentalized; that is, teachers are specialized in subject matter, and students move from teacher to teacher, rather than remain in the same room all day. In an attempt to meet the transitional nature of the students, paricularly in the seventh and eight grades, certain subjects are frequently grouped into core programs, such as English and the social studies. This calls for a teacher who is especially equipped and trained to handle the combination. For the most part, however, the

---

18 For more comprehensive coverage, see Robert Beck, Walter Cook, and Nolan Kearney, *Curriculum in the Modern Elementary School,* 2nd ed. (Englewood Cliffs, N.J.: Prentice Hall, Inc., 1960).

19 For more comprehensive coverage, see Wm. Van Til, Gordon F. Vars, and John H. Lounsbury, *Modern Education for the Junior High School Years* (Indianapolis: Bobbs-Merrill Company, Inc., 1961). While the Junior High School is an established phenomena in American education, it is by no means universal. Many school systems are organized on the 8–4 basis, in which eight grades comprise the elementary school, and the ninth grade is incorporated into the high school structure.

junior high school teacher is prepared much the same as his high school counterpart.[20] In fact, in some schools when both levels are housed in the same building, certain members of the teaching staff are interchanged.

The high school. The American high school has been called a unique educational institution. It accepts all the youth from its community, regardless of intellectual level, social background, or their avowed educational purpose, and it is comprehensive in its attempt to provide programs to fit the needs of this broad clientele.[21]

A student enters the American high school at age 15 on the average. From this point, the learner must make specific plans to prepare himself for whatever route he proposes to follow as an adult. The more complex the society becomes, the more critical becomes the guidance and counseling function of the secondary school. Roughly, three general routes must be considered: (1) The academic pattern that will best fit the plans and needs of the student. Here, the choice hinges on the probable point of termination of formal education and the beginning of productive contribution to society. If the student, on the one hand, chooses to terminate his education with high school graduation (as some 60 per cent of them do at the moment) at about age 18, some attention must be given to vocational possibilities and the abilities that make entrance into the working community a realistic venture. On the other hand, if the choice indicates that additional study in college is needed for entrance into one of the professions or into graduate work, the emphasis must be maintained on scholarly talents and academic performance. (2) The pattern of experience indicated for personal development. Here, physical development, social development, and the value orientation of the student are considered, along with a pattern of courses that will help him to understand some of the nonacademic factors in life, and how he may adjust himself to them. (3) Finally, an extracurricular complex of experiences is available, ranging all the way from living and studying in foreign lands to public performances in music, drama, and athletic events.

The concern in this discussion is not with current arguments over

---

[20] In most institutions, however, he can major at either the elementary or secondary level.

[21] For more comprehensive coverage, see Wm. Alexander and Galen Saylor, *Modern Secondary Education* (New York: Holt, Rinehart & Winston, Inc., 1959).

the relative weight given to the three areas outlined above. The purpose is to try to reflect the flavor of the American secondary school as it exists, and for which teachers must be trained. There are two very significant features of this agency. One is its flexibility—the dynamic that exists within the American high school which makes it most sensitive to a wide range of student needs and national and cultural directions, as contrasted to the rigidity and narrowness in scope of its counterparts in other countries. Again, the comparison is not made as either favoring or discrediting the American model, but to characterize its uniqueness. The second feature, and perhaps a more important factor, is the development of the American high school as almost an indigenous society within the broader scope of national culture. Gradually, as the nation has moved into an industrial and economic pattern which virtually eliminates gainful employment for youth under 17 years of age, the high schools have evolved a complex of experiences to fill the gap. Here, the "teen-agers," as the student body is called, find a world of their own which provides a relatively secure and satisfying environment. Along with the basic program of classes for intellectual and educational growth, there is a carefully planned schedule of social, cultural, and even simulated political experiences. The youth involved become almost totally immersed in this whirlwind of activity. The pattern has been criticized as unrealistic, given too much to pampering youth, and even anti-intellectual. The evidence at present, however, while giving some credence to these criticisms, is not sufficient to establish them. The saving grace of the system is its built-in flexibility and sensitivity, which make possible a rapid adjustment to correct the critical weaknesses that develop.

It is within this pattern that secondary teachers in the United States work and make their contribution to the development of the nation's youth. The training institutions must look to the pattern in designing the educational programs for its teachers.

Programs of Preparation

The teaching staff of the American school system numbers over 1,500,000. Each year approximately 150,000 new teachers must be supplied to replace those retiring or leaving the profession, and to service the growing enrollment.[22] More than 1100 colleges and universities are now organized to provide teacher education for the new recruits, and they are also equipped to give additional in-service education to those already certified.

The variation in types, organization, and internal structure, along with some philosophical differences, has already been outlined in this chapter. Within this framework of difference and structural contrast lies a rather sharp composite model for teacher education that is remarkably consistent from institution to institution.[23] It is a pattern of core areas in the curriculum, and that pattern appears in a number of organizational situations. Although there are variations, the general components are common to every program in the country. The areas are as follows:

1. Breadth in academic background and general education.
2. Depth in an area of specialization in some academic discipline.
3. A sequence of professional courses.
4. A series of laboratory experiences or practicum.

Emphasis may be placed at different points; that is, more attention may be given to general education than to the specialized area, or vice versa. The general program and the specialized areas may be cut back to accommodate more time for professional courses, or (as is happening in many institutions currently) the professional courses and laboratory experiences are being sharply curtailed in order to provide much more depth in the student's major concentration. These emphases tend to ebb and flow with the needs or pressures of the moment; but the general package has remained the same for many years, and it gives every evidence of continuing for the forseeable future.

Academic background and general education. Requirement of a broad academic background and general education is universal. It is predicated on the assumption that a teacher must be a broadly educated person. Institutions vary only in the extent of general

---

[22] See *Review of Educational Research,* Vol. XXXIII, No. 4 (October 1963), 355–66.

[23] Based on the study of over 100 programs in different and varying types of colleges and universities. The material was taken from the college catalogs and faculty self-study reports of these institutions.

courses required, in where the emphasis is placed (humanities vs. physical science or social science), in the patterns by which general education is organized, and in the quality of the offerings. For the most part, the general program will consist of from 40 to 60 semester hours, or from one third to one half the total four-year curriculum. English is basic; six hours of composition is common, and one or more courses in literature will normally be included. The social sciences constitute another block; the traditional pattern stresses American and/or European history and political science, along with electives in sociology, anthropology, geography, general psychology, and economics. Lately, however, there is a noticeable trend toward more emphasis on the behavioral sciences. Practically every institution requires some grounding in the physical and biological sciences and in mathematics. Many include study in one or more foreign languages. The fine arts, especially speech and music, receive considerable attention, and most institutions require basic work in physical education. For the remainder, a student, with his adviser, may select supplementary electives in any of the above areas, or in any course allowable in his institution that may strengthen and broaden his background.

Table 1 shows in considerable detail how four different kinds of institutions organize the program of general education in the teacher education curriculum. It should be noted that this sequence is taken regardless of the area of specialized concentration the student will follow. Hence, candidates preparing for elementary school teaching will be required to follow the sequence of general courses, as will students majoring in a subject area for junior or senior high school teaching.

Although the general format is the same for each program, there is a variation from pattern to pattern. For example, the single-purpose college has placed stress on integrated, survey-type courses —as in the nine-hour block called the "Basic Course in Humanities," or the three-hour course in "Contemporary World Cultures." No mathematics or foreign language is required in this sequence. A sampling in three areas of science is indicated, and the strongest emphasis is placed on the social sciences, with 19 hours of requirement.

TABLE 1

PROGRAMS OF GENERAL STUDIES IN FOUR KINDS OF PREPARATION INSTITUTIONS[24]

Subject-Matter Areas	Single-Purpose Institution*	Four-Year Liberal Arts Institution*	Multipurpose Institution†	Graduate School of Education
Humanities	English Composition Basic Course in Humanities	English Comp. 5 English Lit. 10 Religion 9 5 Fine Arts 5 Foreign Lang. 20 (If student has no high school background in foreign language)	English Comp. 6 hours required Six hours to be chosen from at least two other fields, including: 1. Literature (either English or foreign language 2. Philosophy 3. Historical or theoretical courses, philosophy, music, art, speech, or drama Three hours to be selected from nonhistorical or theory courses in speech, drama, art, dance, music	Since all students have earned the baccalaureate degree at entrance, they are expected to have completed the general requirements before admission. The Ad-

Social Science	Genl. Psychology 5 Personal Living & Community Health 5 Individual & Social Relations 3 American Life & Institutions 3 Contemporary World Culture 3	Twenty hours to be chosen from at least two fields: History Economics Political Science Sociology	Nine hours to be selected from two areas: Anthropology, Economics, Geography, History, Political Science, Psychology, Sociology	missions Committee examines all records carefully and may refuse admission to a student not having adequate general preparation, or it may require deficiencies to be made up.
Laboratory Science	Physical Science 3 Biological Science 3 Earth Science 3	Eighteen hours to be selected from two fields: Biology, Chemistry, Physics, General Science	Six hours to be selected from: Biology, Botany, Chemistry, Geology, Geography, Physics, Zoology	
Physical Education	Six hours required in first two years	Six hours during first two years	Four hours required in first two years military science may be substituted	
Elective			Six hours in addition to above in: Foreign language, Science, Mathematics, Social Science	

* Given in quarter-hours credit; to get semester-hour equivalent, take ⅔.
† Given in semester-hours; add ½ to get quarter-hour equivalent.

24 Material in this table and following outlines abstracted from the official 1963 catalogs of the Colorado State College of Education, Greeley, Colorado; Hiram College, Hiram, Ohio; Harvard University, Cambridge, Massachusetts, and the University of Nebraska, Lincoln, Nebraska.

The liberal arts college is typical of a prescribed program of general studies without too much flexibility. The English and humanities area is designated rather rigidly. Some choice is given in the social sciences, but it must be confined to two areas. The same is true in science. This pattern requires from 70 to 90 quarter-hours, depending on how much foreign language the student had in high school.

The multipurpose university allows flexibility on the part of a student and his adviser to sample rather widely, or to concentrate with considerable depth in an area in which the student is weak. In this case, the program can be almost tailor-made to fit the needs of the student.

The graduate school has no program of undergraduate instruction; it assumes that the student has met this demand in the pre-entrance undergraduate degree. The admissions authority analyzes all transcripts and makes the decision on the balance and/or depth that is found in the student's academic background.

Depth in an area of specialization. A distinction in requirements for depth of specialization must be made between the programs preparing students for elementary and secondary school teaching, for the two patterns differ rather markedly. The major area for the elementary teacher is really "elementary education," which means that considerable knowledge needs to be attained in all or most of the subjects taught to elementary school youngsters. The elementary teacher is expected to instruct in the language arts, mathematics, social studies, and the sciences. If the pattern in the school is completely self-contained, whatever is done in music, art, physical education, and even foreign language will also be taught by the same teacher. The elementary teacher in training is so busy with a program that gives a nominal background in all the subject areas that it is virtually impossible to work out a major in depth in any single one of them. Some institutions, however, are now attempting to develop, if not an academic major, at least one or two general areas of academic emphasis, such as mathematics and science (both biological and physical), English and the humanities, or relatively broad coverage of the social sciences.

The elementary major. The four following outlines show in detail how each of the different kinds of institutions listed in Table 1 fashion the elementary major.

The Pattern for the Elementary Major in a Single-Purpose Institution

General Requirements, 42 quarter-hours (see Table 1)

Elementary Art	5
Music Fundamentals	2
Music Methods and Materials for Elementary Teachers	2
Physical Education Activities for the Elementary School	2
Health Education in the Elementary School	2
Teaching Science in the Elementary School	3
Arithmetic for Elementary Teachers	3
Teaching Handwriting and Spelling in the Elementary School	2
Improvement of Instruction in Reading in the Elementary School	3
Improvement of Instruction in English in the Elementary School	3
Improvement of Instruction in Arithmetic in the Elementary School	3
Improvement of Instruction in Social Studies in the Elementary School	3
Literature in the Elementary School	2
Reading in the Primary Grades—or	
Reading in the Intermediate Grades	3
World Geography—or	
Anglo American	5
Unit Survey of United States History	5

48 quarter-hours

Elementary Education majors are required to earn either a minor of 27 quarter-hours or to earn 15 quarter-hours in each of two areas of concentration, one of which must be in the Division of Humanities, Social Studies, or Sciences. The Chairman of the Division offering the minor area of concentration will determine the courses required.

The Pattern for the Elementary Major in a Four-Year Liberal Arts College

General Requirements, 69–89 quarter-hours (see Table 1)

Elementary School Health and Physical Education	6
Music Literature and Appreciation for the Elementary Teacher	3
Music Education in the Elementary School	3
Arts and Crafts in the Elementary School	3
Teaching Elementary Social Studies	3
Childrens' Literature	3
Language Arts in the Elementary School	3
Teaching Elementary Foreign Language	5
Teaching Elementary Science	5
Teaching Elementary Arithmetic	5

39 quarter-hours

Academic work beyond the major includes 24–40 quarter-hours to be determined by the student and his adviser, and will be designed to strengthen the general proficiency of the student.

The Pattern of the Elementary Major in a Multipurpose University

General Requirements, 42 semester hours (see Table 1)

Teaching of Reading	3
Teaching of Art	2
Teaching of Social Studies	3
Teaching of Language Arts	3
The Elementary Curriculum	2
Childrens' Literature	3
Early Childhood Education	4
Elementary Science	3
Elementary School Mathematics	3
	26 semester-hours

In addition to general requirements, 24 additional hours in academic work must be taken. The selection of specific courses is made on the basis of the student's need for additional depth in an area, or if he wishes to show special strength in some field.

The Pattern of the Elementary Major in a Graduate School of Education

General Requirements, a Baccalaureate Degree (see Table 1)

Since all students who enter this School of Education have already completed the baccalaureate degree, the pattern is considerably different from those described at the undergraduate level. Several programs are available. The following outline indicates the courses to be taken by a student who has no elementary teaching experience but who is a candidate for the Master of Education degree, with specialization in Elementary Education.

Two half-courses in the principles of teaching and supervised teaching.
One half-course in the language arts in elementary education.
One half-course in social studies, art, and music in elementary education.
One half-course (elective) to be chosen in consultation with adviser.

If the student is experienced in elementary teaching, then the program becomes very flexible, including a required half-course in the principles of teaching and four half-course electives to be chosen with the adviser from courses appropriate to the candidate's professional and academic plans.

As noted in the foregoing outlines, the elementary major in each of these institutions is concerned mainly with the organization and the teaching design for the subject matter of the elementary school curriculum. Hence, the teaching of elementary arithmetic, science, or language arts, for example, receives special attention. This, however, is more than teaching methods in these subjects. It is a review and analysis of the subject matter itself, along with the format for organization of the material for presentation, and alternate designs for teaching it.

The secondary major. The secondary or high school teacher will generally specialize in a subject discipline represented in the high school curriculum, such as English or mathematics. Some fields are somewhat generalized—for example, the social sciences, which include a combination of courses in history, political science, economics, sociology, geography, and perhaps anthropology. Following are outlines that show how the different types of institutions fashion programs of major concentration in the field of English.

The Pattern for the English Major in a Single-Purpose Institution

English Composition (five quarter-hours required in general education sequence)		
Shakespeare		3
English Poetry from Chaucer to Milton	3	
The Restoration and 18th Century	3	
The Romantic Movement	3	
Victorian Prose and Poetry	3	
Contemporary English and American Literature	4	12–13
American Literature to the Civil War		4
American Literature since the Civil War		4
Creative Writing I	2	
Creative Writing II	2	
Creative Writing III	2	 2
Advanced Grammar and Syntax		2
Advanced Expository Writing		3
The English Language		4
Literature and Materials in the Secondary School		4
History of Ideas in English Literature		3
Elective Courses in English		7
		48–49 quarter-hours

This is an example of a program which is almost completely prescribed. Of the 48 quarter-hours in the sequence, the student is allowed only seven hours of elective courses. There is a balance between the study of literature and an opportunity for the student to do some writing of his own. As a contrast, in the following pattern for the liberal arts college a great deal of flexibility is permitted, but the program is almost entirely devoted to literature.

The Pattern for the English Major in a Four-Year Liberal Arts College

English Composition (five quarter-hours required in general education sequence)

Introduction to British Literature I		5
Introduction to British Literature II		5

Representative British Plays I	5		
Representative British Plays II	5		
History of the English Language	5	Student chooses	
Shakespeare I	5	five hours from	5
Shakespeare II	5	this block	
Seventeenth Century Period	5		
Milton and His Times	5		
American Life and Literature I	5		
American Life and Literature II	5		
Restoration and 12th Cen. Literature I	5		
Restoration and 12th Cen. Literature II	5	Student chooses	
Poetry of the Victorian Period	5	five hours from	5
Nineteenth Century Prose	5	this block	
Poetry of the Romantic Period	5		
Nineteenth Century Novel	5		
Twentieth Century English and Am. Lit. I	5		
Twentieth Century English and Am. Lit. II	5		
Masterpieces in English I	5		
Masterpieces in English II	5		
Masterpieces in English-Honors Course I	5	The student and his	
Masterpieces in English-Honors Course II	5	adviser select an	
Imaginative Forms of Prose I	5	additional	35
Imaginative Forms of Prose II	5	35 hours	
Renaissance Nondramatic Literature	5	from the	
Chaucer	5	total block	
American Thought I	5		
American Thought II	5		
American Thought III	5		

55 quarter-hours

The English major in the multipurpose university is somewhat less restricted than that in the single-purpose institution, but more so than that in the liberal arts college. It places considerable stress on writing, and it adds one speech course which does not appear in either of the other patterns.

The Pattern for the English Major in a Multipurpose University

Beginning Composition (taken in the general education sequence)		6
English Composition	3	
Advanced Composition	3	3
Critical Writing	3	
Literary Composition	3	
Types of British and American Literature I	3	6
Types of British and American Literature II	3	6
Survey of English Literature I	3	6
Survey of English Literature II	3	6
American Literature I	3	3
American Literature II	3	
Shakespeare I	3	3
Shakespeare II	3	
Seventeenth Century Literature I	3	
Seventeenth Century Literature II	3	
Restoration and 18th Century Literature	3	
Nineteenth Century Novel	3	
Early Twentieth Century Novel	3	
The Romantic Movement I	3	
The Romantic Movement II	3	
Major Victorian Poets	3	9
Nineteenth Century Essayists	3	
Continental Fiction	3	
Continental Poetry	3	
World Literature I	3	
World Literature II	3	
Medieval Continental Literature	3	
Continental Novel	3	
Speech Education in High School	3	3

33 semester-hours

The graduate school of education does not list a course pattern for any major. Since the students who matriculate for work in teacher education already hold a baccalaureate degree, they will have previously completed a subject-matter major. This is carefully analyzed by the faculty. If the major is not satisfactory, the student will not be admitted, or he will be asked to strengthen his program by taking additional courses.

The Professional Sequence

The professional courses offered in every program of teacher education are designed to develop the attitudes and competencies which presumably result in effective teaching. Attitudes, as well as abilities and methods, are included as significant objectives. The sequence will generally include a block of courses in what has come to be known as "Educational Foundations," or sometimes the "Social and Psychological Foundations of Education." The general content of this area will include the history of education in Western civilization (especially in the United States), the role of the school in the American social order, the philosophies that have developed about and around education, and the psychology of human growth and development. The material is incorporated into a number and variety of courses. Increasingly, basic study in psychology, philosophy, sociology, and sometimes in anthropology is required as prerequisite to the more specialized courses in education.

In addition to the foundations area, a pattern is included which has come to be known as "methods courses." Actually, these are courses involving the practicum of teaching. They are rightly concerned with methodology, but they also place major attention on the format for teaching. The student learns how to plan his teaching design. He is required to observe experienced teachers and to analyze what they do. Much attention is given to the motivation of students to learn and to the means for evaluating their progress. An attempt is made to show the wide variation in the intellectual capacity and environmental background of the students. Experience is also given in organizing the subject material into teachable units. The student is shown how to use instructional aids, such as models, laboratory equipment, charts, graphs, maps, and a variety of audiovisual devices that have been developed for use in the classroom.

Finally, the practice-teaching experience, done under supervision, requires the student to demonstrate his ability as a teacher. Some colleges maintain their own campus schools for this purpose, but most student teachers are assigned to regular schools for periods ranging from six weeks to a semester. More and more, the student-teaching experiences are being extended into a form of internship. The practice is not yet fully developed, but it may become standard within a few years. At present, no particular pattern is discernible except for a gradual extension of the student-teaching experience, which sometimes takes the form of a semester or even a year of probationary teaching before the training institution gives its final endorsement.

Table 2 shows the professional sequence patterns offered by the four kinds of institutions.

Laboratory experiences. The student teaching and observation required in the standard course patterns are laboratory experiences. In addition, most of the training institutions require or encourage a variety of activities designed to supplement the formal class program. It is virtually impossible to structure these as a part of a given institution's program, because they are not rigidly scheduled and are usually informal. In general, three categories of experience are found.

First, students observe children of different types in a number of different situations. Opportunity is given to see children and youth in the actual school situation at different grade levels, in formal classrooms, at play, and in various activities. Students in preparation are also encouraged to visit different types of homes to study the various kinds of environments and backgrounds. They are advised to note child-parent relationships, along with the interrelations of children in the homes. These experiences become points of reference which the student in education can use in the seminars and formal classes in his training program.

Second, students are encouraged to engage in a series of experiences in the broader community environment. They may visit ameliorative institutions such as orphan homes, orthopedic hospitals, and special schools for the physically and mentally handicapped. In addition, they may study how a community provides recreational activities for its children and adults. In general, it is hoped that the future teacher may get the "feel" of a community by watching its various functions in action and by engaging in a number of its activities directly.

Third, since a teacher is a professional functionary, the student in training is given a number of experiences to acquaint him with the world of professional activities. The National Education Association has established an affiliate for students called the Student NEA. Chapters are rapidly appearing on many campuses. Students learn the objectives and the operations of the parent organization. At the campus meetings of the association, an attempt is made to simulate the problems and issues that will be met when the prospective teachers become professionals. In addition, a student may select from a number of other, more specialized, professional student or-

TABLE 2 PROGRAMS IN THE PROFESSIONAL SEQUENCE OFFERED IN FOUR KINDS OF INSTITUTIONS

Area	Single-Purpose Teachers College*		Four-Year Liberal Arts College*		Multipurpose University†		Graduate School of Education
The Foundations of Education	Basic Concepts of Education	5	General Psychology	5	One semester course to be chosen from:		‡ ½ course to be chosen from each of three areas: History of American Education
	Educational Psychology	5	The School in American Society	5	Introduction to Teaching	3	or Introduction to the Philosophy of Education
	Philosophy of Education	5	Human Development and Learning	5	The Foundations of Modern Education	3	or Modern Thinkers and Educational Issues
			Education Evaluation	5	or Introduction to the Philosophy of Education	3	or Topics in the History of American Education ½
					or The History of Education in the U.S.	3	Psychology & Measurements
					Two courses to be chosen from:		or The Psychology of Human Learning
					General Psychology	3	or Development of Personality and Social Behavior
					Human Development & Behavior I	3 6	or Introduction to Education Anthropology
					Human Development & Behavior II	3	or Introduction to Educational Research
							or Test Construction ½

PROGRAMS IN FOUR KINDS OF INSTITUTIONS (Cont.)

Area	Single-Purpose Teachers College*		Four-Year Liberal Arts College*		Multipurpose University†		Graduate School of Education	
Methodology and Design	Introduction to Student Teaching in the Elementary School or Introduction to Student Teaching in the Secondary School	3	Secondary School Methods	3	General Methods	5	Contemporary Issues in American Education or American School—The Social Foundations or Sociological Analysis of the School System	½
	Methods of Teaching in the Secondary School or Elementary Subject Content Methods	§	Elementary Subject Content Methods		Methods in the Secondary Teaching Major	§	Curriculum and Methods in the Special area of Teaching	½ 3
					Elementary Subject Content Methods		Principles of Teaching and Supervised Teaching	½ §
Practicum	Student Teaching	12	Student Teaching	12	Student Teaching	8	One summer practicum teaching. One academic year of internship.	

*Quarter-hours; take ⅔ for semester-hour equivalent. † Semester-hours; add ⅓ for quarter-hour equivalent.
‡ ½ course equivalent to 3 semester-hours. The sequence shown here for the graduate school of education is derived from the Master of Arts in Teaching pattern. § Courses taken in the elementary major sequence.

ganizations. Among these are the Association for Student Teaching, the Association for Childhood Education International, and several other groups associated with subject areas.

The student advisers in the training institutions attempt to balance the laboratory activities between observation, visits, community activities, and professional groups. If this is done carefully, a student's formal and academic program can be greatly enriched.

The Students in Teacher Education

Over half a million students each year are in training to become teachers in the United States. Many more thousands return to the training institutions each year for additional work toward more advanced degrees, or in programs to upgrade their certificates or otherwise to improve their professional performance or status.

Some controversy has developed, not only as to how well these students are being prepared, but also regarding the quality of person selected to enter the program. Are the training institutions content to admit inferior material, and then do nothing to weed out the incompetents during the process of training?

To answer such questions categorically is impossible, because a wide range of selection policies exist in the many institutions preparing teachers. As a matter of fact, the answer depends on where the answer is sought. Some collegiate institutions have virtually no entrance standards, except high school graduation. Others accept only those with very high qualifications. The University of California, which enrolls only the upper 12½ per cent of the high school graduating class, starts with superior material. Other institutions vary, with cutoff points at the fiftieth or the seventy-fifth percentile, and so on. In some cases students are admitted on the basis of examinations, and in others various instruments such as interviews and recommendations are used.

Equally varied are the retention policies. The practice of requiring a minimal average course grade to stay in college is almost universal, but here again the minimum is different from place to place. A "C" average in one institution may actually represent a higher standard than a "B" at another. Similarly a cutoff point on an entrance examination is meaningless until one knows the particular norm of the examination and what universe of students is used as a base.

The National Council for the Accreditation of Teacher Education requires that every institution it accredits establish criteria for admission, retention, and graduation. The criteria relate not only to academic performance, but also to other areas, such as speech proficiency, physical and mental health, and proficiency in communication (particularly English usage). Here again the practices vary widely, and it is difficult to strike any kind of a valid mean.

Perhaps the only index that makes any kind of sense at all is the trend in upgrading preparation from the very beginning of organized teacher education in the United States. In 1800 virtually no schooling was required in order to teach, although this must not be interpreted to mean that all or a majority of teachers were without schooling. A few were fairly well educated for the times; and many others, who had no formal education, had mastered the fundamentals by themselves, or via the apprentice route. Since there were no certification requirements, a teacher had only to convince the employer of his competency.

By 1850 certification laws were beginning to have an impact. Although the situation remained spotted all through the nineteenth century, a gradual tightening of requirements is noticeable. It is extremely difficult to pinpoint a definite time when a given plateau was reached, because requirements varied so widely from state to state and, for that matter, within each state. A rough guess would indicate 1890 as the time when graduation from the eighth grade was minimum for any kind of teaching. High school graduation became minimum preparation about 1900, or certainly by 1910. Some college work for elementary teachers became the mode after World War I, and generally the baccalaureate was considered minimum for high school teaching. At present the baccalaureate is the mode, with some states certifying elementary teachers with less than college graduation, but only as a starting point. Renewal of the great majority of certificates requires additional college work, and almost all permanent certificates require the degree.

In addition, graduate work is requisite for renewal of many certificates. A number of states require the fifth year, and the master's degree is becoming a quite common qualification for teachers.

Although the quality is not yet sufficiently high, it must be pointed out that in the next half-century the training institutions must more than double their output of teachers. If, at the same time, they must sharply upgrade the quality of their programs and the standards of entrance and retention, the task will indeed be formidable. They will have to compete for talent from a restricted manpower pool of quality people. The other professions and the growing demand for superior research personnel will be drawing from the same source. In addition, the problems of staffing with adequately prepared faculty personnel complicate the responsibility. The achievements may have to fall somewhat below the desired expectations.

The Trend in Teacher Education Programs

There is a format that is followed quite closely by training institutions in teacher education. It consists of four areas: (1) A pattern of general education courses required of all students regardless of their major or area of concentration; (2) a sequence of courses to obtain depth in a major subject area if the student wishes to teach at the secondary level, or a broader spread over the whole spectrum of subjects taught to children in the grades if the candidate wishes to become an elementary teacher; (3) a sequence of professional courses that include foundations in educational history, philosophy, sociology, and psychology, and some courses in methods to give practice in planning the teaching units and designing the methods of approach; (4) a series of formal and informal laboratory experiences with children and youth, which will culminate in a supervised teaching experience or in an internship on the job. Both of the last-named are carried on in an actual school situation.

There is no indication at present that any major changes will be made in this general format, but emphasis within the pattern seems to be shifting rather markedly. More depth in subject matter, particularly for secondary teachers, is being stressed. Subject majors are appearing in some elementary programs in place of the former emphasis on the so-called professionalized content courses, such as "arithmetic for the elementary school," or "elementary language arts." As yet, these shifts are mainly quantitative; that is, more courses in the major are included, or academic courses are added to the elementary sequence. This is done under the easy assumption that including more academic work produces a better teacher. As the institutions develop more experience and maturity in evaluating their programs, they may revise this assumption somewhat. They may prefer to concentrate on the appropriateness of the academic offerings in achieving a satisfactory balance between superior scholarship and superior professional teaching competence.

Another change in emphasis is in the structuring of the professional sequence. One departure from the traditional pattern concentrates all, or almost all, the practicum and related courses into a single semester or year. In this plan the courses in psychology that are concerned with learning and human growth and development are scheduled concurrently with the student-teaching experience and the study of methodology. In short, the student is exposed to a package of professional courses concentrated within a relatively short period, so that he can cross-reference theory and practice and see the relationship firsthand. At present there is no evidence that this practice actually produces better teaching performance, although it does have some obvious administrative and teaching advantages.

A second experiment that has received considerable national attention is the growing practice of placing the student in training in a school as an apprentice. He learns the practicum of his profession on the job under the watchful eyes of both the supervisors from the training institution and the professional teachers in the school. An attempt is made to synthesize his experiences in a series of seminars with his supervisors. Here, he and his fellow apprentices engage in informal discussions of problems, methods, and individual progress. Not enough evidence is available to establish any real superiority for this approach, but it appears to have some definite merit.

CHAPTER III

The Current Situation—Certification

Licensure of certain functionaries within the structure of the society has become a standard practice. In fact, it has existed almost from the beginning of civilized cultures, and in some instances it can be found operating at a crude level in some cultures that can scarcely be called civilized. The general purpose is simple—to allow certain individuals to perform particular functions for which they must demonstrate special aptitudes, beliefs, skills, education, or whatever the society has established as necessary for the protection of its members or the promulgation of its heritage. The structure through which the licensing is accomplished and the manifold needs that licensure is supposed to serve or protect can be quite complex and confusing.

The licensing of teachers is almost as old as organized society, and it perhaps involves as much or more complexity than any other area where licensure is practiced. During the sixth century B.C. in Athens, the schools were placed under state supervision. This was appropriate to the Athenian point of view, for the state assumed considerable responsibility for boys between the years of six and eighteen, and teachers were licensed accordingly. A different reason lay behind the certification of teachers in the early European societies. The growth of the church and song schools made it impossible for the "scholasticus" and "precentor" to serve except to train and supervise the song or parish teachers of the diocese. By 1150 a centralized system for the licensing of teachers had been established, and an oath of fealty and obedience was required.[1]

Early Patterns

The English people who developed the New Amsterdam Colony in 1664 required a license for teachers as a guard against the em-

---

[1] E. P. Cubberley, *The Certification of Teachers,* 5th Yearbook, National Society for the Scientific Study of Education (Chicago: University of Chicago Press, 1906), p. 176.

ployment of religious dissenters. As long as the religious groups retained some autonomy, they maintained the specific church faith requirement.

As late as 1760, the qualifications established by the governor of New Jersey specified that to obtain a license to teach, one must be of good character, loyal principles, and professed protestant faith. The religious emphasis declined slowly, but the quality of loyalty became a heated issue as the colonies took on a more national character, and as the issues that brought about separation were beginning to emerge.[2]

The colonial attempts to license teachers met with varying degrees of success and failure. The paucity of well-prepared teachers, the difficulties in communication and in supervising the enforcement of standards, and the increasing religious divergencies present in some of the colonies hampered the task of licensing. All through the colonial period the authority for licensing teachers was vested in the civil authorities, and thus a precedent was established for instituting the state as the agency of major responsibility in licensure. While the church wielded considerable power in the process, it did so, not as a matter of right, but because it was able to influence the public officials.

As the people of the colonies became more heterogeneous and more mobile, the growing population migrated to new areas and the churches lost some of their influence. The religious emphasis remained, but it was more general and less doctrinaire. Character and disciplinary virtues were substituted for orthodoxy. Academic requirements had begun to appear by 1840; qualifications were judged by lay persons who varied in their abilities to evaluate. Jacksonian Democracy and frontier independence generally supported the concept of lay evaluation, which with the advent of boards of education became a second echelon of responsibility, under the state, for establishing regulations to ensure that those who entered teaching were qualified.

Late Nineteenth-Century Developments

In the rather permissive atmosphere of the last half of the nineteenth century, a miscellany of subgovernmental agencies—town-

[2] *Ibid.*, p. 41.

ships, towns, and counties—either assumed or were granted some prerogatives in certification. Mostly, certification was by local governmental personnel, and as often as not the authority was first appropriated and later legalized, as the states got around to the task of setting up their educational machinery.[3] At the time of the Civil War, a number of licensing agencies and a great deal of variation existed. California (Law of 1864–65) presented a curious blend of old, new, and developing trends in certification.[4] There were three district boards of examiners: state, county, and city. Each had power to grant certificates for certain grade levels and of specific duration validity. In effect, this provided for a graded plan of certification. Although the city certification was valid only in the city of issuance, considerable reciprocity existed. Moreover, what some considered long overdue recognition was given the graduates of state normal schools. Graduates of these institutions were not required to take the same examinations as the professionally untrained, but were certified on the basis of completing the institution's approved program.

Most states continued throughout the century to reserve to local school officers, such as county and town superintendents, the right to certify teachers. In a few states, such as New York, the State Superintendent had granted some licenses prior to the War Between the States. Gradually, however, more centralization began to appear. State superintendents or commissioners were appointed, or elected, and were granted the authority to conduct examinations, evaluate the results, and grant teacher certificates valid on a statewide basis. This movement, which began in the last decades of the nineteenth century, accelerated and gained its greatest momentum after 1910. State, county, and local examinations were gradually dispensed with, and more attention was given to the completion of courses (often quite specific) in academic and professional areas.

---

[3] All through the nineteenth century, particularly in the newer states, adequate educational legislation and school codes had to await the pleasure of the legislative bodies. Frequently, they would adopt school codes, place them on the statute books, and forget about them; or at best they would supply inadequate funds for their enforcement. As a result, the situation nationally was rather a "catch as catch can" proposition before 1900. See W. K. Beggs, *"Frontier Education in Nebraska,"* Doctoral dissertation, University of Nebraska, Chap. II, 1939.

[4] Elsbree, *op. cit.,* p. 190.

Evolution of the Modern Systems

Adequate and accurate treatment of the evolution of teacher certification in the United States after 1900 would require that each state be discussed separately.[5] The provincialism that started in the colonies, and that was maintained in the formative years of the republic, diminished only slightly, if at all. State patterns perhaps became somewhat more sophisticated, but nothing approaching uniformity appeared in the amount or nature of preparation for the teaching license, in the number or kinds of certificates granted, or in the duration of their validity. States which generally have shared a comparable economic, geographic, and historic status have developed quite divergent systems of certification. Modifications and innovations were likely to come at different times by legislation or by the administrative action of state departments of education. Moreover, in some of the states teacher certification was delegated to several subunits of government, so that wide variations developed within the state itself; for example, a certificate good in one county might be invalid in the adjoining county.[6]

Even so, strong undercurrents were beginning to appear in the confused procedures and patterns of certification. Gradually, the states began to reclaim the prerogatives of licensure as a state-level function. Pressure from the colleges, the profession, and the public were resulting in upgrading practices. Stronger academic and professional preparation were demanded, along with a better definition of each type of certificate and the necessary qualifications to secure it.

Centralization of authority. In 1898 only three states had completely centralized the licensure function. By 1903 the number had increased to five. Fifteen states had adopted the practice by 1921, thirty-six by 1926, and thirty-nine by 1933. In 1950 Massachusetts was the lone state with diversified authority, but during the next year a total revision of its certification laws was begun. Not only was the authority centralized, but also a process of upgrading was adopted,

---

[5] *Ibid.*, pp. 336–7.
[6] E. W. Knight, *Fifty Years of American Education* (New York: The Ronald Press Company, 1952), p. 330.

which would require that by 1954 all teachers in Massachusetts hold at least a baccalaureate degree.[7]

Armstrong and Stinnett indicate the continuing tendency in state legislatures to fix complete responsibility at the state level.[8] The trend is moving away from legislative prescription of the details. General policies and frameworks are adopted, but the actual spelling out of requirements is left to state boards of education. By 1961 almost all the states had given partial or even complete autonomy to the state boards, or departments of education, for establishing requirements, for original issuance, for renewal, and for the revocation of certificates—within the framework of statuary provisions. The legal provisions were generally quite nominal, indicating general age ranges, character, citizenship, oaths, health, and sometimes special courses, usually relating to state factors of geography, history, and government.

In 1961, however, state boards were still denied autonomy in certification procedures in Colorado, Indiana, Nebraska, North Dakota, and Puerto Rico. Ten states allowed certain exceptions, as shown in Table 3.

It will be noted in Table 3 that the exceptions are usually attempts to protect the vested interests of a unit of government, certain colleges, or teacher groups.

Upgrading practices after 1900. For reasons that are not yet apparent, the turn of the century appears to be the point at which most of the states began to look seriously at the educational background of the persons who were being certified to teach. This is not to imply that no improvement was in evidence before 1900. Actually, the teachers associations, the colleges and normal schools, and some boards of education were exerting pressure for upgrading the quality of both teaching competence and educational background. Furthermore, many potential and practicing teachers were taking additional high school and college work on their own initiative. Most of the legal agencies, however, did not convert these demands

---

[7] *Ibid.* See also R. F. Butts and L. A. Cremin, *A History of Education in American Culture* (New York: Holt, Rinehart & Winston, Inc., 1953), p. 453.

[8] W. E. Armstrong and T. M. Stinnett, *A Manual on Certification Requirements for School Personnel in the United States* (Washington, D.C.: National Commission on Teacher Education and Professional Standards, National Education Association, 1957), pp. 11–12.

TABLE 3
EXCEPTIONS TO COMPLETE AUTONOMY IN TEACHER CERTIFICATION
BY
STATE BOARDS OF EDUCATION

State	Legislature	State Board	State Board and other Agencies
Delaware		x	x[1]
Illinois		x	x[2]
Kansas		x[3]	
Maryland		x[4]	
Missouri		x	x[5]
New York		x	x[6]
North Dakota	x		x[7]
Oregon		x	x[8]
Pennsylvania		x	x[9]
South Dakota		x	x[10]

[1] City of Wilmington.
[2] City of Chicago.
[3] Kansas is required to grant one certificate to Bachelor of Science in Education graduates of the three state colleges.
[4] City of Baltimore has, by law, been excepted from state certification and certain other state requirements.
[5] The five state colleges, Lincoln University, and the University of Missouri are impowered to grant life teaching certificates to their graduates being granted the degree of Bachelor of Science in Education. Third-grade certificates (valid one year) may be granted by county superintendents on the basis of examination.
[6] The cities of Buffalo and New York certify their own teachers; all teachers, however, must be certifiable by the state commissioner of education.
[7] Special legislation has provided for three cities to certify their own teachers; one does so. Persons holding diplomas as graduates from state colleges in education are accorded certification.
[8] Any school district over 100,000 population may certify. Portland qualifies under this law, but requires its teachers to receive state certification if they wish tenure.
[9] Emergency certificates valid for a short amount of time may be issued by county or district superintendent.
[10] For junior college teacher certification only, the University of South Dakota issues certificates.

and trends into law until after 1900, and the real advancement came after 1910.

Even then the process was painfully slow. By 1910 a number of the states were setting high school graduation as a minimal requirement, but as late as 1921 30 states still had stipulated no specific educational background, although examinations were given in most instances to establish at least some academic proficiency. Fourteen states required a minimum of four years of secondary school (not necessarily graduation), and four required high school graduation. This was a minimum requirement for full certification. The requirements for temporary or emergency certificates were less exacting.[9]

Armstrong and Stinnett have traced the establishment of the degree requirement, baccalaureate level or above, as it has appeared since late in the nineteenth century.[10] As would be expected, the degree (or degrees) were first required for high school teachers. Utah established the policy in 1896. California adopted the requirement gradually between 1896 and 1900, and added a fifth year of college work as basic in 1905. The District of Columbia made college graduation mandatory in 1910. Then, slowly the other states followed suit. In 1920 ten states in all had adopted the practice. By 1930, thirteen more had been added, and by 1940, forty were requiring college graduation of some sort. By 1950 college graduation was a standard prerequisite to begin secondary teaching in all the states.[11]

The pattern was different for the elementary teachers. It was not until 1930 that college graduation was established as minimum for the lowest level certificate, and then only one state and the District of Columbia adopted the requirement. Not until after World War II did the practice become general. In 1945 eighteen states required the degree, and by 1961 forty-four had initiated the baccalaureate minimum for any kind of an initial certificate.

Presently, the situation remains roughly as it was in 1961. Six states and Puerto Rico still allow one to start teaching with less than a college degree. These exceptions are as follows:

1. Maine, which requires 96 hours.
2. Mountana, which requires 64 hours for the Provisional Certificate. The Provisional Certificate is granted upon graduation from an approved two-year program and is renewable if evidence exists of preparation toward the Standard Certificate (bachelor's degree).
3. Nebraska is in the process of altering certain aspects of teacher

---

[9] Elsbree, *op. cit.*, pp. 347–52.

[10] Armstrong and Stinnett, *op. cit.*, 1961, p. 10.

[11] *Ibid.*, pp. 3, 24–25. See also Elizabeth H. Woellner and M. Aurilla Wood, *Requirements for Certification*, 28th ed. (Chicago: University of Chicago Press, 1963, pp. 1–4). This, however, leaves a wrong impression. Practice was well ahead of state requirements. The regional association would not accredit a high school after 1920 unless most of the teachers had degrees. Local requirements in most of the larger schools were well ahead of state regulations. Actually, after 1920 college graduation was the rule rather than the exception for high school teachers.

certification; the changes will be announced in 1964. By most recent standards, Nebraska requires elementary rural teachers to have 40 hours and elementary town teachers to have 60 hours.

4. North Dakota requires 64 hours.
5. Puerto Rico requires 68 hours.
6. South Dakota requires 30 hours for rural school teachers and 60 for town teachers.
7. Wisconsin requires 64 hours.

California, which has always taken the lead for advancing requirements, has moved beyond the baccalaureate degree minimum. On July 1, 1963, it initiated a minimum of five years of college for any Standard Teaching Credential. An elementary teacher, however, can be initially employed on the basis of a partial fulfillment of qualifications, and may complete the fifth year within five years. Connecticut, Kentucky, and Washington have roughly comparable procedures.[12]

All states require the bachelor's degree for certification of secondary teachers, but there are some loopholes. For example, West Virginia, by law, will no longer issue a secondary certificate on less than the bachelor's level of preparation, but the State Board of Education may issue temporary certificates to teachers who do not meet the degree qualification. The trend is to go beyond the basic degree. Arizona will allow two years of high school teaching on a bachelor's degree plus six hours of graduate work. When the teacher has earned an additional 18 hours of graduate credit, the certificate may be renewed for two years; the permanent secondary credential requires the master's degree or 30 semester hours of graduate credit. California and Washington also require five years of preparation. Although New York issues a provisional secondary certificate in the academic areas on the basis of the bachelor's degree, there is a five-year validity limitation. The certificate is not renewable, but is to be followed by permanent certification upon the completion of six additional graduate credit hours in education or the subject field. The Oregon regulations provide a provisional certificate on the basis of the bachelor's degree; standard certification requires that a fifth year be completed within five years of the issuance of the provisional certificate. Much the same situation exists in Washington, except that six years are allowed for the completion of the fifth year. In

---

[12] Woellner and Wood, *op. cit.*, pp. 17, 23, 60, 142.

Indiana and the District of Columbia a fifth year, including a master's degree, is required for the permanent certificate.

Temporary and emergency certificates. The military requirements of World War II siphoned millions of men and women out of their normal occupations and into the armed services and related war work. The teaching staff of the school system was badly depleted. After the war, many former teachers did not return to the classroom. To make matters worse, the output of new teachers was reduced to a fraction of the normal flow. Before the schools recovered from these restrictions, the population explosion began to increase enrollments sharply. As a result, the nation has experienced a serious shortage, not only of qualified teachers, but also (in some instances) of poorly prepared personnel. To fill the gap, certification agencies have issued temporary or—as sometimes called—emergency certificates.

The practice is neither new nor necessarily harmful. The qualifying terms "emergency" or "temporary" do not always imply inferior quality. The recipient may lack only one or two specific requirements. He may be short of the requisite academic or professional college hours, or he may have allowed a once valid certificate to lapse. Abuses have occurred and will probably continue to occur in licensing persons who have substandard qualifications or who lack attributes required by law, but it is difficult to see how the schools could have survived the war and the subsequent postwar dislocations without the teachers who held emergency certificates.

Both inside and outside the profession, much concern has been expressed about the impact of emergency personnel on the general quality of the school programs. Whatever the effect, the problem is becoming less acute. In proportion to the total number of teachers employed, the percentage of substandard certificates has dropped steadily since 1945. The ratio has improved from one emergency certificate for every seven regular certificates in 1945 to one in 15 by 1961 (or 6.7 per cent in the latter year compared to 14.3 per cent in 1945).[13]

Number and types of certificates. Since the beginning of teacher licensing in the United States, many grades, types, and qualities of certificates have been issued. It should be pointed out that

---

[13] Armstrong and Stinnett, *op. cit.,* 1961, p. 23.

presently the states do not grant a license just to teach. The recipient is certified to teach at the elementary or secondary level; if he is to teach at the latter level, the subject or subject areas are endorsed. Generally, however, the states defer to the training institution for the endorsement, although they frequently specify the number of hours to be completed in a given subject and sometimes indicate specific courses to be taken.

The variation in detailed practice among the states is so wide that it is virtually impossible to draw specific generalizations. Certain broad categories can be shown, however. One classification is based on the duration of validity. For many years a so-called "life certificate" was granted by most of the states. These were valid until revoked for cause. The earliest record of their authorization was in New York state in 1843. By 1921 almost all the states issued life certificates.[14] Since that time, the practice has gradually been discontinued, although not completely, and a type called the "permanent certificate" has been substituted. This credential is valid as long as the recipient either teaches continuously or does not let a specified number of years lapse without teaching. Other terms sometimes applied to this type of certificate are "continuing," "standard," or "professional." In some instances, a teacher's license will remain in force only as long as he upgrades his competency in his teaching field by additional study. Several states issue provisional or probationary certificates, which are valid from two to six years, during which time the teacher must complete requirements for the next higher certification level. The emergency certificate is generally limited to one year.

The level of preparation defines a second classification of types. For example, an initial certificate is granted when the baccalaureate degree is completed along with the proper requirements. Renewal is based on the addition of completed study, generally at the graduate level. Through the continuous process of adding more course hours, the recipient may move through one or more renewals to a permanent or continuing certificate. The initial certificate may be prestandard, provisional, limited, or probationary, depending upon what the state chooses to designate as the beginning level.

The third category includes certificates which define the subjects,

---

[14] Elsbree, *op. cit.*, p. 346.

areas, or levels to which a teacher may be assigned. Several types belong to this classification, including the general certificate which allows teaching in any area or at any level. Cubberley wrote in 1906 that "in almost all of our states a teacher's certificate of any grade is good to teach in any part of the school system in which the teacher may be able to secure employment."[15] Currently, however, only 16 states retain this certificate; even in these states it does not give the teacher carte blanche as it did in 1906. Although the certificate may not specify level or area, other legislation will prescribe what is required to teach in a given subject or field. Some of the states control teaching assignments by refusing to accredit a school that consistently assigns teachers to fields or levels for which they were not prepared according to law.

In the early years, states would issue "special certificates" for teaching in such areas as language, music, art, penmanship, or perhaps in the kindergarten. Others would specify different levels such as primary grades, intermediate grades, or high school. This practice has been generally discontinued, although two levels, elementary and high school, are generally recognized. The emerging practice seems to be the issuance of a general certificate with an endorsement for a particular level or special field(s). The endorsement is generally made by the training institutions, but in some instances the state endorses upon the recommendation of the college. Practices vary from state to state, but currently 41 states issue certificates which endorse the academic teaching field. A few still issue special certificates of varying kinds, and two (Vermont and Maine) endorse the teaching area(s) only when the candidate does not meet the qualifications for a standard or full certificate.[16]

Requirements in specific course preparation. As educators generally have placed more and more stress on the academic preparation of teachers, this emphasis has been reflected in certification requirements. The trend now is definitely toward minimum course requirements both in academic and professional areas. Some states specify the basic hour minimums. Others approve college programs and make the stipulations in the approval standards. Table 4 shows the composite of these requirements for seven subject areas which pertain to all certificates, either elementary or secondary.

---

15 Cubberley, *op. cit.,* p. 59.
16 Armstrong and Stinnett, *op. cit.,* 1961, pp. 16, 54–56.

TABLE 4

A Composite of Certification Requirements in all the States
for Seven Subject Areas (in Semester-Hours)[17]

Subject	Range		Mode	Average
English	B	15–48	24	25
	M	6–36	24	20+
Modern Language	B	15–48	24	23—
	M	6–36	18	18+
Mathematics	B	12–40	18	21—
	M	6–30	18	17—
General Science	B	12–40	24	22+
	M	6–32	18	18—
Physical Sciences	B	8–40	*15,24	23+
	M	6–40	15	16
Biology	B	8–30	24	20—
	M	6–24	18	15+
Social Science	B	15–54	30	27+
	M	6–54	24	23—

* Bimodal distribution.   B = basic requirement.   M = minimum requirement.

The requirements in professional education courses range from 16 to 36 semester-hours for the elementary certificate; the median number of semester-hours required is 21, while 22.4 hours constitute the average. At the secondary level the range in semester-hour requirements is from 16 to 36; the median is 18 hours; and the average is 19.[18]

Reciprocity in Certification

Where each state has autonomy to set up its own teacher licensing practices as it will, the movement of teachers from one state to another can be greatly impeded. In fact, at times some of the states have adopted punitive measures as a sort of tariff wall to keep out-of-state trained personnel from competing with the home-state teachers. This has really never been too serious, because there was

[17] *Ibid.*, pp. 20, 61.
[18] *Ibid.*, pp. 26–27. See also D. L. Barnes and C. D. Shipman, "Teacher Certification," *Education Digest*, 27 (1962), 7.

generally a way to subvert the restriction, although the "foreign" teacher generally paid something of a penalty in the process.

With the rapid population increase, the shortage of teachers, and the growing mobility of the population, the necessity for free movement of teachers from one state to another has become critical. Since American educators always have been opposed to national laws or regulations in such matters, the states have resorted to cooperative reciprocity arrangements. Most of them have an extralegal flavor, but to date they have worked fairly well. Armstrong and Stinnett report two regional reciprocity compacts now in operation, an 11-state arrangement in the Northeastern section of the country, and a compact composed of seven member states in the central region.[19] The *Journal of Teacher Education* for December 1961 published a map of the United States showing the 27 states which have accepted for certification purposes any graduate of a teacher education program accredited by the National Council for Accreditation of Teacher Education, with the stipulation that certain specific requirements of the receiving state be met.[20]

In all, 35 states have established some kind of a reciprocity arrangement. The situation is not entirely satisfactory, but it is relatively easy now for a teacher educated in one state to move to another for his teaching. In fact, for some states this has become the rule rather than the exception.

The Trends in Certification Practice

Considerable emphasis has been placed in this account on the diversity of types and procedures in teacher licensure. Although diversity remains the prevailing situation, certain trends seem favorable both for the quality of teachers and for a reduction of the provincialism that has characterized the operation. The trends are:

1. An over-all upgrading of preparation. In some states this amounts to working toward the bachelor's degree requirement, while in others the candidate must move toward five years of preparation or the master's degree as a maximum requirement. Furthermore, the upgrading is rapidly

---

[19] Armstrong and Stinnett, *op. cit.*, pp. 17–18.
[20] National Council for Accreditation of Teacher Education, *Journal of Teacher Education*, 12 (1961), 448.

developing an increase in the quantity and/or quality of teaching-field preparation and in improving the quality of professional course experiences.

2. The use of certification as a level of sophistication. Instead of issuing a multiplicity of certificates (one state has reported 65) for specific fields and grade levels, certificates tend to reflect varying degrees of preparation. The first full certification will probably be *limited, probationary,* or *provisional* of prescribed validity duration, contingent upon completion of certain hours or the fifth year. Advanced certification will be designated as *permanent, continuing, regular, standard,* or *professional* of extended duration. For the most part, the older type of "life" certificate will disappear. A few states still grant them, but the requirements are rather demanding. For example, Alabama requires the candidate to be within one year of the doctor's degree; Indiana requires 10 years of teaching experience plus the master's degree. Finally, as the trend veers away from specific requirements, the pattern is returning to the general or blanket type with some type of endorsement for acceptance in a given teaching area.

3. Reduction of specific course requirements. States tend to make fewer specific requirements and to leave this decision to the institutions within the general framework of an "approved program."

4. An increase of the influence of professional groups of varying kinds in the adoption of policies relative to certification. Most of these are extralegal advisory groups, which may represent all levels of professional practice from college down to kindergarten, and a broad array of subject or area specialization. Two states, Colorado and Indiana, have created special boards or commissions to serve in a consultative capacity. The board in Colorado consists of eight members, each of which must be actively engaged in some educational enterprise. In Indiana, a Commission of six members has been appointed, four of which must be practicing teachers.

5. Forty-seven of the states have created a broadly representative body composed of teachers, administrators, and faculty from the training colleges, and of various lay organizations which have an interest in education, such as boards of education, Parent-Teacher Associations, and even some self-styled "improvement associations." These advisory agencies are usually legally sanctioned, but they have no authority in either legislation or administration. They do serve, however, as valuable sounding boards and recommending agencies for the legally constituted authorities who must make the final decisions relative to certification.

As a general summary of the directions in certification practice, it may be noted that there is no disposition to take the final authority away from state officials. There is, however, a definite trend in broadening the scope of influence in the development of policy. In

other words, state legislatures and officials are looking less to their
own devices and wisdom in certification matters, and more to a
broad spectrum of problems, issues, influences, and national needs
as the bases for final decisions. This will probably result in some
major changes in the nature and number of certificates, and in the
general structure and procedure in licensure.

The Issues in Certification

A great deal of the tension that grows from dissatisfaction with
the American school system and the teachers that serve it is centered
in the problems and issues involved in certification practices. Most
of the critics will not take the time to learn the origins of existing
practices, the evolution of the system, or the involved factors that
make teacher licensure a complicated problem at best. Nevertheless,
issues are apparent, and there is a great deal of clamor for improvement. Roughly, the issues fall into four categories: (1) Centralization vs. decentralization; (2) the role that should be played by the
training institutions; (3) the place of the teaching profession in
certification; (4) approved programs accredited by a national body
such as the National Council for Accreditation of Teacher Education; and (5) a miscellany of suggestions from a variety of persons
and sources.

Centralized vs. decentralized authority.   As long as the traditional structure in American government remains as it is, the basic
authority for the issuance of a license to teach must remain at the
state level. There is, however, nothing in the constitutional provisions
of the various states, and certainly not in the federal Constitution,
that would deny state legislatures or officials the privilege of dele-
gating the authority. Although no one is confused as to the seat of
authority for the final decision, there is considerable conviction that
much more responsibility should be placed in the colleges that prepare teachers, and in the organized profession to police its own
ranks in the process of upgrading competence. The most radical
departure from present practice would suggest that the states grant
only an over-all certificate to teach, without reference to level or
area of teaching. It would be left to the integrity of the training institution to specify what it had trained the candidate to do and at
what level. The responsibility for placement within a school system

would then rest with the board of education and its administrative staff. The professional associations would be alert to spot members teaching in a field or at a level where they do not have adequate competence or preparation, and to take whatever disciplinary action is deemed necessary. Such a procedure would make the state little more than the approving agency for a process which lies largely outside its jurisdiction. Most, if not all, the state governments would probably refuse to move to this extreme. There are, however, many gradations of possibilities between complete prescription by the state and delegation of most or all responsibility to other agencies.

The role of the training institutions. One of the possibilities is inherent in the relationship of the state to the colleges that prepare teachers. This relationship is itself an issue. Should the state have the authority to prescribe to the colleges the type and the extent of the programs they must offer in order to have their graduates certified? Probably no state wishes to exercise such prerogatives to the point of controlling college curriculums, and certainly no college faculty would willingly accept such dictation. The alternative is a cooperative attack on the problem. Assuming reasonable agreement to general objectives, the college can then set up its programs accordingly. The state may approve the programs *in toto,* or it may suggest alterations, additions, or adjustments, thus reaching a working compromise. Or, the state may set up such general standards as "adequate academic preparation"; it would then trust to the integrity of the college in writing its own definition of "adequacy." The relationship can be quite flexible and permissive, or it can be semiformal, with carefully delineated channels of responsibility and prerogatives. The state authorities have the choice of working with each college in the state, approving each program separately, or reaching a compact with all the colleges as to general requirements, again trusting that each college will be responsible in the development of specifics.

The development of a working relationship between state officialdom and the training colleges can be greatly abetted by the establishment of state commissions or committees on teacher education. These function as delegate assemblies and can provide a number of services—for example, to find facts, to develop ideas, to frame recommendations, and to serve as liaison between the various groups and agencies involved in the certification process.

The place of the profession. The teaching profession has substantially matured in the past few decades. As a result, many of its members believe that it is no longer necessary for teaching certificates to be as detailed and varied as they have been. Although basic responsibility should be retained by the state, the individual teacher is usually a responsible professional person. As such, he does not need the patronizing care of the state to outline all the steps he needs to take in order to maintain and improve his proficiency. Moreover, he desires a voice in the establishment of the policies and procedures by which he is licensed to practice his chosen profession. He feels also that, in concert with his fellow teachers in professional associations, adequate safeguards can be established to protect against any defections by individual members.

The organized profession maintains that teachers are willing and eager to join forces with the training and employing agencies and with the state in working out the details of the process by which they will be licensed. Furthermore, the profession is ready and capable to establish professional standards and ethical practices, and to see that its members live up to them.

Approved programs accredited by a nationwide agency. At the center of many of the present dissatisfactions, not only in certification but also in teacher education generally, is the issue of nationwide accreditation of teacher education programs. When an autonomous agency, such as the National Council for the Accreditation of Teacher Education, accredits certain college programs, and when the states accept these programs as approved for certification purposes and as a basis for reciprocity, then the autonomous agency is prescribing the basis on which persons may enter the teaching profession. This, so the contention goes, gives entirely too much power to an extralegal body, especially when it is not responsible in great degree to the broad interests it professes to serve. It is further argued that the NCATE is unduly influenced by the National Education Association through its Commission on Teacher Education and Professional Standards, and by the American Association of Colleges for Teacher Education. These agencies are presumed to favor professional courses over academic preparation.

Actually, most of these charges are without substantial foundation. Some states do use the NCATE accredited programs as one basis on which they will grant certificates without prejudice; but in no case is this the only basis, and the other states make no reference to NCATE at all. Moreover, the NEA influence is more imagined than real, and the TEPS Commission is adamant in its demands for much more academic depth in the preparation programs. Finally, AACTE is composed of over 600 institutions, many of them liberal arts colleges, and it numbers many of the prestige colleges and universities in its ranks. If AACTE has a strong bias toward professionalism and tends to downgrade academic preparation, it is certainly without the blessing of these institutions. The fear of national accreditation on the current basis persists, however, and it may be so strong that approved programs can never be successfully used as a basis for reciprocity in certification.

In summary, it may be assumed that the teacher certification situation in the United States is in a fluid state. In most respects this is as it should be. Much progress has been made, and more is in prospect. Certainly, no one would desire that the situation be crystallized on one or two methods or procedures.

CHAPTER IV

The Current Situation—Accreditation
of Programs in Teacher Education

In 1939 a group of 26 accrediting bodies was called together in Washington by the American Council on Education to discuss the growing concern of many university presidents over what they considered the encroachment of educational accrediting bodies into the control and government of the nation's schools and colleges. The concern was stated in the Introduction to the proceedings of the conference:

> Another reason for recent interest in accrediting grows out of the restrictions which these agencies have placed on local control of the educational program. Though the requirements imposed by individual accrediting agencies may be no more rigid and exacting than they were several decades ago, the total effect of their prescriptions is materially greater. Trustees, administrative officers and faculty members have, therefore, begun to wonder who really controls our educational institutions. They see final determination of educational policy consciously or unconsciously being assumed by accrediting agencies and they are exercised by what they consider a usurpation of their own legal and proper responsibilities.[1]

Growth of the American System
of Voluntary Association

The problem faced by the Council in 1939 was not new, and it was not fully resolved at this meeting. The situation concerning accreditment of almost every kind of educational program and institution in the country is the result of a peculiar historical development in the United States—the continuous striving of educators for what might be considered a unique form of "having their educational cake and eating it too." In other words, they have tried to maintain local control or institutional autonomy, and at the same time they have

---

[1] American Council on Education, *Coordination of Accrediting Activities,* Series I, Vol. III, No. 9 (1939), p. 1.

tried to develop and apply some form of quality regulations to ensure relatively high standards.

President Samuel P. Capen of the University of Buffalo summarized the situation in his address to the 1939 Conference:

> Those who study what we choose to call the American Educational System cannot fail to be surprised that so vast an organism can have developed without any plan. There has, of course, been detailed planning in abundance. There have been projects by the thousand. But there has never been a plan. And viewed in the large, the American educational system is still a mass of inconsistencies and dislocations. . . . Elementary and secondary education had separate origins and have not yet been related to each other. Higher education grew up independently and has never been satisfactorily related to secondary education. Professional education passed through its infancy and adolescence as an orphan child. It did not have any connections . . .
>
> Everybody knows the reason for this most essential characteristic of American education. . . . Education in America is a state function, not a national function. . . . But when we say that education is a state function in America, we really mean that it is a local function. Few states have exercised effective control of education within their borders.[2]

Capen noted that the American people through voluntary taxation and unparalleled private generosity have built the most diversified and extensive educational complex in the world:

> But it was not ever thus. . . . We had colleges, so-called, and universities, so-called, and schools of medicine and law, again so-called, that were travesties upon the names they bore. We had entrance requirements for publication only, and not for application to candidates for admission. We had commercial exploitation of students. . . . We had fraud. And perhaps worst of all we had . . . gross ignorance of the standards appropriate to institutions of higher education.
>
> The situation cried out for reform and the instrument of reform that we devised was altogether consonant with the genius of our institutions. . . . We did not appeal to an outside agency like the state to rescue us. We took on the task ourselves. Our instrument has been called voluntary standardization. . . . The leaders of higher education and the leaders of some of the older professions collaborated in defining the minimum standards which, in their judgment, should be met by colleges or by professional schools. They inspected

---

[2] *Ibid.*, p. 5.

existing institutions, using these standards as criteria for judging material resources, and published the results of their observations.[3]

Thus, as Capen so aptly explained, the leaders in American education invented a technique for establishing realistic standards and a method of applying and enforcing them. The process is not necessarily an unmixed blessing, because the standardizing associations tend to multiply both in numbers and in strength. While the leaders in education may help to create a system of voluntary standardization and endorse it by submitting their institutions to the inspection and classification involved, they may also revolt and call the accrediting associations to an accounting for any real or imagined abuse of the prerogatives granted to them.

Actually, the whole complex of accrediting agencies that has grown up in the American educational system is a shrewd, although intricate, system of consensus voluntarily arrived at, and an equally intricate system of checks and balances to keep the educational machine in some sort of equilibrium.

The alternatives are governmental control and inspection on the one hand, and educational anarchy on the other. American educators have, thus far, avoided retreating to either extreme.

Voluntary Association in Teacher Education

Standardization of any kind, either voluntary or imposed, is based on some type of evaluative criteria. These generally evolve out of the established or stated objectives of the enterprise under consideration. Where the objectives are at issue, it is perfectly possible for separate groups, starting from the vantage points of separate value orientations, to come up with startlingly different standards as the measuring sticks which ought to control what goes on in the operation. The orientations may evolve from tradition, conviction, or (as is becoming more and more the case) from careful study and research.

At the moment, the most that can be said for the standards applied to teacher education is that they are a combination of all three, with increasing emphasis on study, research, and revision; but the progress up to this point has been tortuous indeed. Starting as a

---

[3] *Ibid.*, p. 6.

secondary school function—with the established collegiate agencies remaining entirely aloof from, if not hostile to, the whole operation —the teacher education leaders began to upgrade their institutions through voluntary associations; they affiliated rather naturally with the infant National Teachers Association (later called the National Education Association), which maintained a division of Normal Schools from its inception more than a century ago.[4]

Standardization Efforts in the Normal Schools

The impression must not be given that the Department of Normal Schools was a standardizing agency, or that it made any attempt at standardization. It was rather a marshaling ground where those interested in teacher education could gather to discuss and exchange ideas and practices, and to maintain a repository for their records and proceedings. The normal school adherents, however, were not without issues. Wesley noted three viewpoints that were issues in the early years.[5] All concerned the programs of preparation. The majority accepted what was then called the academic viewpoint. The entering students, even those from the high schools and academies, were woefully weak in even the elementary knowledge of grammar, arithmetic, geography, and other studies which they would be expected to teach, and it was necessary to bring them up to a reasonable level of information in these areas. After what was considered a thorough grounding in content, the students received some instruction in the principles of education; they read whatever was available to them in the theory and practice of teaching, such as Page's treatise by that title.

A second group stoutly maintained that the preparation of teachers should not be academic. They argued that it was a professional process and that the entire program should be treated as such. Hence, while subject matter would be a most important part of the curriculum, it should be knowledge to be taught, not just knowledge to be learned. "The future teacher was thus learning history [for example] and at the same time he was consciously selecting materials and organizing them for future classes of his own." Subject matter, as a

---

[4] Edgar B. Wesley, *NEA—The First Hundred Years* (New York: Harper & Row, Publishers, 1957), p. 88.

[5] *Ibid.*, p. 84.

result, was learned and learned to be taught, all in a single operation. Moreover, "only the normal school understood the necessity
for this kind of instruction." There was a touch of naïve arrogance
exhibited here, but it was combined with an equally shrewd insight
into a process that even yet remains the basic structure for teacher
education.

The third point of view professed that the normal school should
have nothing to do with academic preparation at all. Only those with
a thorough substantive background should be admitted, and the
curriculum should be confined almost (if not entirely) to professional preparation or, as they would style it, to the "science of education and the art of teaching."

Although these positions appear to be somewhat oversimplified,
anyone familiar with the modern scene in teacher education will
immediately recognize the three component issues as center-stage
properties that still characterize the teacher education drama. Had
there been an accrediting agency in the mid-nineteenth century, one
can well imagine how the standards would have differed had the
proponents of each viewpoint been asked to write criteria for the
evaluation of teacher education at that time.

There was, however, no accrediting agency in the nineteenth
century. Instead of standardization, a sort of competitive anarchy
seemed to prevail. Wesley stated:

> A committee appointed to survey normal schools in 1897 and
> 1899 reported that it found distressingly wide variations and the
> lack of any disposition to formulate standards. Instead there was a
> constant disposition to show peculiarities and specialties and to
> oppose others in their notions just as peculiar and provincial . . .
> New England normal schools stressed professional work; the north-
> central normal schools were broader in their programs and more
> influential; there was little agreement on what professional courses
> to teach.[6]

To make matters worse, there were three types of normal schools:
state-controlled, city-controlled, and privately controlled. The last,
with a few important exceptions, were for the most part commercial
ventures with little integrity and practically no scholastic standards.
For that matter, even the better normal institutions in the cities and
states found it virtually impossible to maintain any but the most

[6] *Ibid.*, p. 83.

minimal entrance standards. There were not enough high school graduates interested in teaching, particularly at the elementary level, to fill out enrollments. Moreover, certification standards were so low that an eighth-grade graduate could secure a license to teach by the simple expedient of passing an examination for which he could prepare by studying on his own.

Influences leading to national standardization. From 1850 to 1900 the major emphasis in standardization of necessity had to be a gradual raising of entrance requirements. Just exactly how this was done has never been recorded. Presumably, the desire for status within the normal schools and among the more forward-looking teachers was a genuine influence. The growing desire of the people of the country for more education and greater sophistication in the quality of education available was probably a powerful factor also. In any event, by the turn of the century the normal schools were beginning to require high school graduation for entrance, were taking on some of the appearance of colleges in their own right, and were beginning to call themselves teachers colleges. They had not as yet, however, solved the problem of how to evaluate themselves. As late as January 1917, a small group of teachers college presidents met in Chicago informally and agreed to form an affiliation to be known as the American Association of Teachers Colleges. The first formal meeting of this group was a month later in Kansas City, February 24, 1917. The organization was set up, officers were elected, and plans were made for future activities. Significantly, the main item of discussion was the creation of an honor society of teachers colleges, consisting of institutions offering a full four-year collegiate course leading to "degrees of recognized academic value."

At the second meeting of the association in Atlantic City, February 23, 1919, such an honor society was established, and the first step was taken toward standardization. One year later in Chicago a three-level classification system was adopted. Class A designated those institutions that had already granted degrees; the colleges that had the authority to grant degrees but had not done so were assigned to class B; and the institutions that had four-year courses but no authority to grant degrees were typed as class C.[7]

Apparently it was never intended that this elementary system of

---

[7] American Association of Teachers Colleges, *Sixth Yearbook* (Oneonta, N.Y.: The Association, 1922), pp. 14–16.

classification be any more than* a temporary arrangement, but the major concern had now moved away from entrance requirements to the establishment of a culminating degree, and from this to the type of program that should be followed between entrance and graduation. The early yearbooks are full of the discussions held at annual meetings concerning the need for higher standards and what the specific standards should be. At the 1924 convention, H. A. Brown, President of the State Normal School of Oshkosh, Wisconsin, noted:

> The course of study . . . should be just as well organized with equally exacting requirements of accomplishment and equally excellent instruction as those of the various undergraduate professional schools of the state university. . . . The degree of the state teachers college should be an open door to full graduate standing in the best graduate schools of education in the country.[8]

Brown noted also that there were certain standards which must prevail among teachers colleges before these schools would be entitled to full recognition as institutions of collegiate level. He listed six such standards:

1. Requirements for admission.
2. Organization and content of curriculums.
3. Quality of instruction.
4. Requirements for graduation.
5. Training of members of the faculty.
6. Adequacy of instructional and supervisory staff—in point of number.

From 1917 to 1925, speaker after speaker kept reminding the national conventions of the low level of quality in the preparation programs; and in 1925, the U.S. Commissioner of Education delivered a sharp attack to the assembled institutional representatives, noting in particular the necessity of adopting realistic, but nonetheless rigid, standards. The impression is definitely gathered from reading the association yearbooks between 1922 and 1926 that a deliberate campaign was being waged to condition the membership to accept a specific set of standards and to be judged by them.

The adoption of the first definitive standards. At the Washington, D.C., convention on February 20, 1926, fifteen standards

---

[8] American Association of Teachers Colleges, *Eighth Yearbook* (Oneonta, N.Y.: The Association, 1924), pp. 43–44.

were adopted and defined, and a system was devised to put them into operation. Revisions were made annually for the next five years, until in 1931 a fairly definite pattern had taken shape. The Tenth Yearbook of the Association carries the full text of the standards under the following headings:[9]

1. Definition of a Teachers College.
2. Requirements for Admission.
3. Standards for Graduation.
4. Size of the Faculty.
5. Preparation of the Faculty.
6. Teaching Load of the Faculty.
7. Training School and Student Teaching.
8. Organization of the Curriculum.
9. Student Health and Living Conditions.
10. Library, Laboratory, and Shop Equipment.
11. Location, Construction, and Sanitary Conditions of Buildings.
12. Limits and Registration of Students.
13. Financial Support.
14. Classification of Colleges.
15. Accrediting and Classifying Procedure.

The move toward consolidation of efforts. A careful study of events leading up to the adoption of the foregoing standards, and of the standards themselves, indicates what the leaders in teacher education were attempting to accomplish. The first emphasis was placed on establishing minimums for entrance, graduation, and academic performance that would be acceptable as a collegiate level program. Second, it was hoped that a substantial core of professional courses and practicum could be adopted which would be constant among all teacher training institutions. Finally, there was expectation that an integration and a balance could be achieved between the professional and academic phases of the program.

Although such aspirations seem simple enough now, they were anything but simple in the 1930's. The leaders were dealing with institutions ranging in quality from little more than secondary grade to a few of very high caliber. Moreover, the standards had to cover a wide variety of organizational and legal structures. To complicate the situation still further, the leadership of the institutions ranged from political appointees, who were too often of low caliber, to

[9] American Association of Teachers Colleges, *Tenth Yearbook* (Oneonta, N.Y.: The Association, 1926), pp. 9–15.

highly qualified professional educators. The teaching profession had no organized agency to consider upgrading professional standards, and the academic community remained either aloof or hostile to the whole business.

As generally happens in American education, a number of forces, unseen at any given moment, were beginning to have an impact. Although it would be difficult to document, perhaps the most significant of these was a restlessness that was developing in the faculties of the colleges of teacher education. Generally, this restlessness centered in the multipurpose universities. Here the professional staffs were associating with academic colleagues and were very much disinclined to live out their professional lives as second-class citizens. They wanted students of equal caliber; they wanted their classes and teaching to be equally respected; and they wanted the academic performance of teacher education students to be comparable to at least the median of the total university population. In individual institutions qualities of excellence began to appear, but the process was without any particular reference to other institutions, and it did not represent an across-the-board upgrading.

The regional accrediting associations. Another factor that helped was the growing influence of the regional accrediting associations for secondary schools and colleges. Actually, the impact of these associations had a double effect—influencing both the high school and college levels. For example, the North Central Association of Colleges and Secondary Schools was organized in 1895. It was established ostensibly to develop "closer relations between the colleges and secondary schools." During the early years of its existence, its activities were confined to annual meetings where mutual problems of the two levels of education were discussed and some of the controversial issues were brought into focus. One of the early problems which seemed to defy solution for a time was what classification to give the normal schools. They seemed to be hybrids, part secondary and part college in nature. They were ignored for a time, then given the designation of "unclassified institutions," which satisfied no one in particular. In 1918, they were grouped with junior colleges in a sort of "in-between" category. Finally, in 1935 the Association started publishing its accredited list alphabetically with "specific descriptive designations," which would place each institution on a general scale. In this way the institutions were generally defined as secondary or higher education, but each according to its own pattern and standards of merit.[10]

Standards of a general nature were developed between 1900 and 1910, but the real influence of the North Central Association began with the establishment of three semi-independent commissions on (1) colleges and universities, (2) secondary schools, and (3) research and service. The commissions on secondary schools and on colleges and universities were charged with developing standards for the respective levels of institutions involved, and with applying them to the institutions desiring accreditment. A court case in North Dakota in 1938 established the fundamental legal base for the Association's procedure and rights; hence, the North Central Association became inextricably linked with the educational fortunes of its region.[11]

Almost from the beginning the regulations of the North Central Association had an impact on teacher education. In the first set of standards adopted in 1902, "a bachelor's degree was prescribed for all who taught the so-called academic or college preparatory subjects" in the secondary schools. After 1915 the preparation of the high school teacher of academic subjects "was required to include eleven semester hours in education."[12]

Thus, by imposing certain levels of attainment for teachers and by prescribing certain areas of college preparation, the North Central Association brought its influence to bear on the institutions training teachers. This influence, while indirect, has been nonetheless real, because an Association-accredited high school could employ teachers from only the training institutions which provided the specifics designated in the standards. These standards were constantly upgraded to include administrator preparation and numerous other factors. When one considers that the colleges and universities also desired to be accredited by the Association, and that standards of excellence were required here also, the impact of the associations, as represented by the North Central Association, was indeed impressive. The developments in the other regional accrediting agencies were, in general, parallel to those in the North Central Association.

---

[10] Calvin O. Davis, *A History of the North Central Association* (Ann Arbor, Mich.: The North Central Association, 1945), pp. 23–25.

[11] *Ibid.,* p. 95.

[12] *Ibid.,* pp. 111–13.

Activities of the professional associations.   A third factor which generated considerable influence on teacher education was the combined pressure of increasing certification requirements by the several states and the growing consciousness of professional responsibility within the ranks of the teaching fraternity. The certification story has been covered at some length in Chapter III, and need not be further elaborated here. The professional pattern, however, is quite another situation.

By the midpoint of the nineteenth century enough cohesion had developed among teachers to provide for a national organization. In the ensuing 100 years the National Education Association has evolved into a multicentric body that is almost impossible to define, much less to evaluate in terms of its influence. It is, in fact, now an interlocking directorate which includes representatives of, or organized subassociations for, practically every phase of American education. Some of its affiliates are semiautonomous, such as the powerful American Association of School Administrators, the Associations of Secondary and Elementary Principals, the Classroom Teachers Association, and the Association for Supervision and Curriculum Development. Others are completely independent and are merely housed in the national center in Washington in the NEA building. This latter category includes such agencies as the American Association of Colleges for Teacher Education, or the World Confederation of Organizations of the Teaching Profession.

However organized, and whatever its relationship to the parent body, each of the affiliate agencies has made its influence felt both at the national level and with the group it serves. Each has approached the problem of upgrading teachers and teaching in a different way, but the combined effect has been a gradual tightening of standards, both for state certification and for degree requirements in the training institutions.

Many other factors have been exerting an impact on the total structure of teacher education. Academic groups—such as the National Teachers of English, the American Historical Association, the American Association for the Advancement of Science, and a number of similar groups—have been active. While most of their efforts have been directed toward the curriculum, particularly of the secondary schools, each has had its say as to the kind of teacher necessary to teach adequately in the disciplines involved.

The result, to the layman, must have appeared to be bedlam and chaos, as indeed it almost was—so much so that even before World War II a great deal of thought was given to the possibility of bringing the whole structure of teacher education under one single office for accrediting purposes. It was not until after the war, however, that any real advances were made. The American Association of Teachers Colleges in 1948 merged with the University Deans of Schools of Education and with a similar group from the Association of Municipal Colleges and Universities. The new organization adopted the title of the American Association of Colleges for Teacher Education. This body took over the function of accrediting teacher preparation programs.

In 1950 the AACTE began to accept the liberal arts colleges for membership and to accredit their programs. In addition, a policy was adopted and put into effect which brought state departments of education and various facets of the teaching profession into an advisory relationship with AACTE.

NCATE becomes the national accrediting body. Before the total spectrum of professional and training institutions, lay bodies, and legal structures could be incorporated into the accrediting system, one more step was needed. In 1946 the National Commission on Teacher Education and Professional Standards was organized as a division of the National Education Association. This agency devoted its entire conference in the summer of 1950 to the problem of accrediting programs of teacher education. As a result of this conference, the concept of a national council for the accreditation of teacher education was born and in part formalized. Representatives from the American Association of Colleges for Teacher Education, the National Commission on Teacher Education and Professional Standards, the Council of Chief State School Officers, and the National Association of Directors of Teacher Education and Certification formulated a recommendation for the establishment of the National Council for the Accreditment of Teacher Education.[13]

With subsequent approval of the four agencies and the National

---

[13] National Education Association, *The Professional Standards Movement in Teaching: Progress and Projection*, Parkland Conference Report (Washington, D.C.: National Education Association, 1956), pp. 90–91.

School Boards Association, the first official meeting was held in November 1952. The membership of the Council was as follows:

American Association of Colleges of Teacher Education: 6
National Association of State Directors of Teacher
    Education and Certification: 3
Council of Chief State School Officers: 3
National Commission on Teacher Education and Professional
    Standards: 6
National School Boards Association: 3
                                                     —
                                                    21

July 1, 1954, was the date set for the beginning of NCATE operations. Meantime, AACTE continued to be the national accrediting body for teacher education.

When NCATE became a reality in 1954, AACTE ceased its accrediting activities and became a research and service organization. Its list of 284 accredited institutions was transferred to NCATE as the charter list of accredited institutions, and the latest revision of AACTE standards was accepted to be used for accreditment until such time as NCATE would develop its own, which it proceeded to do with as much dispatch as possible.

The NCATE Standards

The standards adopted by the National Council for Accreditation of Teacher Education consist of seven areas pertaining to the teacher education program of a given institution, for which a complete accounting is required for accreditation. In the introduction to the standards, the National Council notes that "teacher education is and can be effectively carried on in different types of colleges and universities and in a variety of patterns." Furthermore, in applying the standards, "due consideration (must be) given to differences in the nature of that institution, its internal organization, and its curriculum pattern."[14]

The Council also proposes to avoid duplication of effort, wherever possible, by cooperating with regional and professional accrediting bodies and state agencies in the collection of information and in the

---

[14] All references in this section pertain to *Standards and Guide for Accreditation of Teacher Education* (Washington, D.C.: The National Council for Accreditation of Teacher Edulcation, 1960).

general evaluation of the institutions seeking accreditation. Although the Council accredits only those aspects of an institution's program that contribute to teacher education, it fully recognizes that such evaluation must be done within the general setting of the institution; hence, only institutions that meet the following criteria qualify for evaluation:

1. Institutions accredited by the appropriate regional accrediting association at the level for which they request Council accreditation and by the appropriate state department of education for the level and categories requested.
2. Nonprofit institutions of higher learning offering not less than four years of college work leading to a bachelor's degree.
3. Institutions offering four-year curricula (a) for the preparation of elementary school teachers, or (b) for the preparation of secondary school teachers; or (c) institutions offering only graduate or advanced professional programs for school personnel when such institutions provide graduate work in other fields necessary to support these programs.

No effort is made to evaluate the general quality of the institutions under consideration. This is left to the regional accrediting body, which can make its evaluation at the same time or prior to the NCATE visitation.

Each institution is judged on the basis of seven standards: (1) its objectives for teacher education; (2) the organization for teacher education; (3) the student personnel program for teacher education; (4) the faculty for teacher education; (5) the curriculum for teacher education; (6) professional laboratory experiences for school personnel; and (7) facilities and instructional materials for teacher education.

Since the success of the accreditation movement in teacher education will depend on how well these seven criteria enable an institution to describe its program and the Council to evaluate it, a brief analysis of each standard is in order.

Standard I: Objectives for Teacher Education

Two significant factors should be pointed out here. First, the institution is asked to define not only the purposes it has established for teacher education, but also the scope of its operation, and it is asked to indicate how widespread the faculty involvement has been in the formulation of the objectives. Second, the objectives and the beliefs and assumptions on which they are based should be the officially adopted policies of the institution.

Standard II: Organization and Administration of Teacher Education

It is noteworthy that, in this standard, no specific type or pattern of organization is indicated except that at some point, and in some agency, the responsibility for planning, for continuous development, and for evaluation should be fixed as the established policy of the institution.

Standard III: Student Personnel Program and Services for Teacher Education

Here again, no specific pattern is prescribed. The standard, however, calls for a definite system of admission to the teacher education program and retention in it—a system which will ensure a relatively high quality of student at entrance and an equally high performance through the program. A system of records which will identify all students in the program, and the point at which they are accepted in full standing, is also indicated.

Standard IV: Faculty for Professional Education

While no specifics are indicated, it is obvious from reading the standard that the level of preparation, the degree of specialization, and the institution's evaluation of the faculty members for professional education (as to comparative salaries, rank, and responsibilities carried in general institutional activities) will reveal the status of the faculty for professional education.

Standard V: Curriculums for Teacher Education

The general purpose of Standard V is to ensure a reasonable degree of coordination of the course patterns for the prospective teacher. One of the practices that has been prevalent throughout the country for many years allows a student to register anywhere he wishes in an institution, have no particular pattern in the work he takes, elect the minimum number of hours required in professional courses, and thus become certified to teach without a commitment to any particular program. The import of Standard V is to correct this abuse.

Standard VI: Professional Laboratory Experiences for School Personnel

As the standard notes, the capstone of professional laboratory experiences is a continuous, planned, and supervised period of actual teaching experience. Prior to this experience, however, the program is required to provide opportunities for observation of teaching, for working with children and youth in a number of different situations, and for work in community and professional organizations. The avowed purpose of these experiences is to acquaint the prospective teacher with the different types of young people and the social and professional structure in which he will operate.

Standard VII: Facilities and Instructional Materials for Teacher Education

This standard is largely self-explanatory. The strength of any educational program lies partially in the accouterments that are built up around it. In this instance, the buildings, library and laboratory equipment, research facilities and equipment, and especially the unique aids for instruction are significant. In the last-named category of instructional aids, such factors as projection devices, audio equipment, and the various tools involved in all the media of teaching should be available to the students.

How a Training Institution Becomes Accredited

As was noted earlier, at its inception the National Council for Accreditation of Teacher Education accepted the list of institutions accredited by the American Association of Colleges for Teacher Education. It set up machinery to reaccredit these over a period of ten years. In addition, provision was made to consider applications from institutions not on the original AACTE roster. Hence, according to its status, an institution might apply for either initial accreditation or reaccreditation. Actually, the procedure of visitation is much, if not exactly, the same for each type. Each institution must request that it be visited and analyzed for accreditation. The application, however, is optional; that is, no institution is required to subject itself to visitation and analysis. As the accreditation movement has progressed in American education, however, to be on an accredited list is a mark of some distinction and status; to be non-accredited carries the inevitable label of substandard, even though the label may not be correct.

Once the application is received at NCATE headquarters, a chain of events is set in motion, both at the central office and at the requesting institution. These begin to move to a point of convergence on the date of the scheduled visit of the committee to the campus. The headquarters staff mails a set of preliminary instructions, a schedule of costs, an itinerary of dates when the report is due, when and how the visiting committee will be appointed, and a list of bulletins, factual data, and records which must be available to the visiting committee. Approximately six months before the visit, the committee must be selected. A roster of proposed committee members is mailed to the dean or president of the institution, for acceptance or rejection. The local administration has the privilege of vetoing any or all of the proposed list. Once the committee is approved, each member must be notified and his acceptance secured. It should be noted that the members of the visiting committee serve without remuneration and that they receive only expenses. When copies of the institutional report reach headquarters, one is sent to each member of the committee. A chairman is named, who in turn assigns committee members to specific sections of the study and makes arrangements with the administration of the institution as to the conduct of the visit.

When the local institution receives the standards by which it will be judged, another dynamic is set in motion. If the administration of the institution is wise, it will insist that the faculty thoroughly acquaint itself with the standards and determine where they fall short of, deviate from, or square with the criteria. This process is much too long and arduous to describe in detail. Generally, committees are formulated to make the analysis. An over-all steering committee or a director may be appointed to coordinate the procedure.

Eventually, the whole process must culminate in a report. This is generally a rather monumental effort. Although the NCATE admonition is to be brief, most institutions find it impossible to tell their story in less than 100 pages, and many of the reports will reach 300 to 400 pages in length. If the report is well done, it should be both an excellent profile of the teacher education program and a clear outline of the operation of the entire institution.

The Evaluation and Appraisal

The report is due at NCATE headquarters approximately a month prior to the visitation. A copy is sent to each member of the visiting committee. Presumably, each one studies it carefully in anticipation of his particular area of inquiry when he reaches the campus. NCATE maintains four visitation and analysis committees for the purpose of reading both the institutional and the visiting committee reports, and to make recommendations to the Council regarding what action should be taken. The visitation and analysis committee has a number of levels of classification open to it for recommendation to the Council: (1) It may suggest complete accreditation; (2) it may recommend accreditation at certain levels, such as the graduate programs; (3) it may propose refusal of accreditation at any level; or (4) it may defer action. Any institution which is dissatisfied with the decision regarding its status may appeal. Specific machinery has been established for this purpose, consisting of an impartial committee to hear the complaints of a dissatisfied institution. To date, however, no appeals have been registered.

The foregoing explanation of the accrediting process in teacher education via NCATE has been elaborated in considerable detail for a specific reason. NCATE has considerable power, especially if its accredited programs are used as a basis for teacher certification by the states. Also, certain combinations of states are entering into reciprocity arrangements to exchange certificates without prejudice for teachers trained in institutions accredited by NCATE. Finally, boards of education conceivably might consider for employment only teachers who are endorsed by NCATE-accredited institutions. This is a combine of powerful forces. Although no training institution is required to submit itself for analysis, its best interests almost require it to do so if it desires to stay in the teacher education business. As a result, the accrediting standards by which a program of teacher education is evaluated, and the process by which they are applied, are of vital importance to every college and university in the United States, as well as to the entire educational system and the society that sustains it.

This reference to the power inherent in NCATE is not necessarily a criticism of its standards or of the method of their application. Certainly, no accrediting body is of any serious consequence if it does not have the influence to make its decisions felt in the institutions it is accrediting. Whatever authority an accrediting agency has, however, is not legally vested power, but rather the mandate that results from a dispensation voluntarily given it by the agencies it serves. Theoretically, these agencies can withdraw the dispensation at any time they feel that NCATE is abusing its prerogatives; but it is at this point that some serious issues arise, and a great deal of confusion exists.

The 19-member constituent council and the final authoritative voice of NCATE is made up of representatives of six agencies. Ten of the members are chosen from colleges or universities that prepare teachers; three of these represent the National Commission on Accrediting, and the other seven are chosen from the American Association of Colleges for Teacher Education. The Council of Chief State School Officers, the National Association of Directors of Certification, and the National School Boards Association appoint one member each. The remaining six members are selected by the National Commission on Teacher Education and Professional Standards, an affiliate body of the National Education Association. These agencies have a common interest in the kind and quality of teachers that are prepared to teach the nation's children, but that common interest is almost as broad as the total spectrum of American society. When the basic objectives of teacher education are considered, have these six agencies really reached a reasonable consensus as to what the standards should be, and how they should be applied? Moreover, even if consensus has been reached in a general way regarding purpose, does this mean that the Council is equally agreed as to how the general aims should be translated into an administrative structure, a curriculum, a system of student management, and evaluation? Is there agreement as to the best process of providing the essentials of buildings, equipment, libraries, laboratories, and materials of instruction?

When the situation is viewed in this way, the NCATE standards originally adopted by the Council probably represent only a temporary working compromise. They are subject to constant review and eventual revision.

The criticisms of NCATE.[15]   The five most generally expressed criticisms of NCATE and its procedure are summarized below. They are deliberately stated from the point of view of an extreme opponent of NCATE; hence, they may seem somewhat harsh and unreasonable. They do, however, point up the issues.

1. The Council reflects too much the professional point of view. The point is made that the representatives of the TEPS Commission have exerted an inordinate amount of influence, both in the standards and in the way that they have been applied. It is true, so the argument states, that a majority of council members represent colleges, but this is misleading, because the seven AACTE members are essentially professional in orientation and tend to favor the TEPS point of view. In addition, the members from the certification group and the Chief State School Officers are likewise professionally biased; hence, academia is hopelessly outnum-

---

[15] Material for this section was abstracted from correspondence in the author's files and from various articles appearing in the general press.

bered. As a result, the so-called liberal arts point of view is denied an effective hearing in the deliberations of the Council; and teacher education in the United States is drifting off into a milieu of professional methods courses, while academic achievement and serious scholarship are sadly neglected.

2. NCATE should not concern itself with the administrative structure of the training institutions. This is the prerogative of the local administration and faculty. When an accrediting agency attempts to prescribe how a college should be organized to educate teachers, it is usurping the authority of the administration and the faculty. Furthermore, most colleges and universities have evolved a great deal of tradition and certain aspects that are unique to the local situation and its peculiar history. A faculty gets used to, and becomes comfortable in, this framework; to change it abruptly would result in a deterioration of morale, which would offset any advantage gained by changing the administrative structure, even though the change were a considerable improvement.

3. The standards are not applied equally to all institutions. Since the visiting committees differ in personnel, each will have its own complexion, and there can be no standardization of procedure. Hence, an exacting committee may make a good institution look bad, while a careless or indifferent committee will describe a weak institution in such a way that it appears to meet the standards. As a result, a relatively strong institution may find itself provisionally accredited—surrounded in its own region by weaker institutions that have been fully accredited.

4. If the NCATE standards were strictly adhered to, almost all flexibility would be eliminated from teacher education. The claim here is that the standards prescribe one program for teacher education and allow no possibility for deviation or experimentation. There is no best program. An institution should be allowed to maintain several, if it so chooses, and to establish some control mechanisms and measure one against the other.

5. NCATE measures process, not product. By its concern for structure, a common program, student accounting procedures, and the like, NCATE is missing the most important element: the product of the training program. The administrative structure, accounting procedures, and even the curriculum are of little significance when measured against the quality of students that enter the program, the kind of teaching, and intellectual experience students have during the program, and the kind of teachers they become. These elements, not the minutiae, are the ones that should be measured.

The Future of Accreditation in Teacher Education

Although some criticisms of NCATE have been harsh, and in many ways unreasonable, the standards are actually fairly flexible and permissive. The Council has been most diligent in trying to eliminate any real deficiencies in procedure or unfairness in decisions.

An undercurrent of dissatisfaction persists, however, even among some of the strongest proponents of the general concept of accrediting. Recognizing this, the National Council called a conference of 100 people to meet in Chicago in November 1963. This group was broadly representative of every facet of teacher education in the United States, including some of the most vocal opponents of NCATE.[16]

Four analytical papers were read concerning the development, the structure and finance, the procedures, the standards, and the general situation that prevails in the whole NCATE enterprise. The issues were frankly stated and alternate solutions suggested. The group then assembled into discussion groups, and the whole complex of problems and possible solutions was given a thorough airing.

While it is much too early to assess the long-term impact of this meeting, certain tentative conclusions may be drawn. In the first place, the majority of the assembly appeared to be strongly in favor of a national body such as NCATE, representative of roughly the same groups that presently make up the Council, but there were some provisions indicated.

1. The Council must become more sensitive to the wishes, dissatisfactions, varied nature, and local peculiarities of the institutions it accredits.
2. More representation should be given to the organized scholarly disciplines, and to the academic community generally, in the development of policy and procedures.
3. A delegate assembly of all the agencies concerned with teacher education should be called biennially, or perhaps annually, to give reactions, review the general situation, and make recommendations for correction of defects and/or improvement of procedure.
4. The structure of the Council should be changed to give more representation to the colleges that train teachers particularly to the academic divisions of these institutions.
5. The standards should be continuously studied and revised, as indicated by the deliberations and best efforts of all concerned.

The best prediction of the moment appears to be that the National Council for the Accreditation of Teacher Education will con-

---

[16] No report of this conference has as yet been published. The material here has been abstracted from the author's notes made while in attendance at the conference.

tinue with considerable autonomy, but that its prerogatives will be carefully circumscribed by a rather complex and formalized structure of relationships with the institutions it accredits, the profession, the legal agencies, and lay organizations interested in education.

CHAPTER V

The Growing Interest in Teacher Education

The American public, which has esteemed teaching on the one hand as a most important and devoted service, has, on the other hand, been quite casual about how teachers are trained. Since World War II, however, the situation has changed rather markedly, especially in the last decade. A number of factors and forces are involved in the changing attitude: the rising educational level of the population; a growing disposition to listen to college and university faculties in their efforts to upgrade quality in education; and, perhaps most important of all, a growing concern for excellence.

The greatest influence, which no doubt underlies all the others, is the nature of the total dynamic environment in which the American people live. The burgeoning population, the fantastic developments in science and technology, and the competition with the Communist nations have produced severe tensions in American society. These, in turn, have directed some searching inquiries into the nature and quality of the educational system and its teaching staff, and finally to the system of preparation for the teachers. As a result, an unusually receptive national audience has been available for almost anyone who wished to take his turn in addressing himself to the deficiencies of the schools, the teachers that teach in them, and the institutions that prepare the teachers.

Significantly, a growing chorus of voices has been directed to this audience. At the beginning it consisted of dissident elements, each claiming to possess just the panacea to correct all the difficulties.[1] Lately, however, a more moderate and deeper vein of thinking has intervened, less bent on creating friction, but nonetheless concerned with clarifying the issues and initiating some positive reform movements.

---

[1] For example, see Arthur E. Bestor, *Educational Wastelands: The Retreat from Learning in Our Public Schools* (Urbana, Ill.: University of Illinois Press, 1953).

The American Association of Colleges
for Teacher Education

Considerable reappraisal has been conducted within the professional faculties of schools and colleges of education. The National Association of Colleges for Teacher Education, through a special committee, attempted to coordinate this dynamic through the publication in 1956 of a book, *Teacher Education for a Free People*. Although they did not claim to express a consensus of the wide range of thinking that exists within the membership of the Association, the authors tried "to write in such a way as to enlist the interest and attention of both professional educators and lay community leaders who are concerned with improving the quality of the teaching staffs of schools in the years immediately ahead."[2]

The book is largely a reaffirmation of the basic educational elements needed in a democratic society to make it operate effectively. This requires a unique school system, prescribing to some extent the kind of teachers necessary for it and indicating how they should be trained. What exists in teacher education has grown out of a peculiar and rich national experience, and it is deeply rooted in the fabric of the culture. The process should be improved; some changes should be made; and great effort should be expended toward achieving excellence in the product of the training institutions. The basic format, however, is indigenous to the culture and is essentially correct. To change it materially would require a complete reassessment of the fundamentals that have established the direction of the national life.

The Federal Government

The federal government, officially at least, has taken no part in the philosophical or positional struggles in teacher education. Through the acts of Congress in supporting certain activities, and the Office of Education in stressing others, it has wielded some influence, however. Perhaps the most significant early contributions were in the attempts to upgrade the substantive background of teachers in the areas of science, mathematics, foreign language, and

---

[2] Donald Cottrell, ed., *Teacher Education for a Free People* (Oneonta, N.Y.: The American Association of Colleges for Teacher Education, 1956), pp. x–xi.

counseling and guidance. Through the National Defense Education Act, passed August 21, 1958, funds were made available for summer and academic-year institutes, and thousands of teachers were subsidized while in attendance at these. More recently, the categories have been extended to include the humanities and the social studies.[3]

The cooperative research program (authorized in Public Law 531 by the 83rd Congress, and administered through the Office of Education), while not specifically directed to teacher education as such, has made funds available for research into many aspects of education. For instance, grants for analysis of the needs of physically and mentally handicapped children, or grants for the study of the specially gifted, have provided information most useful in the preparation of teachers for these kinds of learners.

Funds for demonstrating the better use of media in teaching, the improvement of English and social studies curriculums, and studies of the mental health of both students and teachers have all provided impetus and encouragement in developing better programs at all levels of teacher education.

The Foundations

The great philanthropic foundations have always had a major interest in the nation's educational problems and have subsidized various ventures involved in teacher preparation. As an example, the George Peabody College for Teachers was originally established with the assistance of philanthropist George Peabody of Massachusetts.[4] More recently, two of the larger foundations have become involved in the issues and problems and, to some extent, have attempted to influence nationwide policies and procedures.

The Fund for the Advancement of Education. In 1951, the Fund for the Advancement of Education was created by the Ford Foundation. This fund began what was to become the most concentrated and best financed effort in the history of the United States to improve and to change the pattern of teacher education. Just where the original impetus for the movement developed is not re-

---

[3] William Alexander and Galen Saylor, *Modern Secondary Education* (New York: Holt, Rinehart & Winston, Inc., 1959), pp. 667–72.

[4] Bulletin, George Peabody College for Teachers, 1963–64, p. 12.

ported, but obviously the foundation made an official policy decision to use its resources liberally to encourage departure from traditional practice in teacher education. It financed a number of experiments, demonstrations, and innovations toward this end.

In retrospect, what the fund proposed to do seems very clear. The Annual Report of the parent Ford Foundation for 1961 indicates the following, relative to the activities of the "fund" in teacher education:

> The programs, which now involve thirty-eight institutions of higher education, seek to achieve a breakthrough in the training of teachers by stressing liberal education and mastery of subject fields. Professional courses are coordinated with paid internships in nearby schools to give trainees extended teaching experience under close supervision. The schools also cooperate in trying out such new teaching arrangements and methods as teaching teams, variations in class size and schedules, and televised instruction.[5]

In another publication of the Ford Foundation, dated September, 1962, this statement appears on the jacket:

> A revolution is under way in the education of teachers. The path to the teaching profession is changing as dramatically as the path to the medical profession changed following the historic Flexner Report on medical education in 1910.
>
> Today's revolution in teacher education is directed to the 100,000 young people who annually enter the teaching profession to help educate America's 40 million elementary- and secondary-school students.
>
> It seeks to redress an imbalance. Under the new pattern, the prospective teacher devotes less of his undergraduate time to courses on how to teach, and considerably more to the academic subject he is preparing to teach. His graduate work consists of even further grounding in academic subject matter, plus studies of the underlying disciplines of teaching: history, psychology, and philosophy. The new teacher's entrance into full-time professional service, like the physician's, is preceded by an internship, which gives him supervised, first-hand experience in teaching a subject he knows.[6]

According to this publication, more than $9,000,000 was granted to 40 institutions between 1951 and 1959 to develop new patterns in the preparation of teachers. Then, in 1959, the real "break-

---

[5] The Ford Foundation, *The Ford Foundation Annual Report*, 1961, p. 3.

[6] Office of Reports, *The New Teacher: A Report on Ford Foundation Assistance for New Patterns in the Education of Teachers* (New York, The Foundation, 1962).

through" was begun—a "series of large grants for more extensive experiments based on these patterns." By September of 1962, fifty-seven colleges and universities had been involved, along with many more cooperating school systems, and the sizable total of $27.5 million had been committed to the effort.

Hence, over a period of ten years the Foundation, along with its cooperating institutions, has initiated a dynamic of rather massive proportions. The beginning in 1951 was, however, quite modest. President Jones of the University of Arkansas addressed a petition to the Fund for the Advancement of Education and requested some $85,000 to "launch a large-scale attack on the problem by setting up and carrying forward a program of teacher education based upon a four-year program of broad liberal education to be followed by a period of combined internship and professional study, as the requirement for certification."[7]

The Executive Committee for the Arkansas Experiment stated in July of 1954 that the main objective of the plan had been the "development of the best possible dichotomized five-year program of studies"—in other words, the separation of the academic and professional segments of the operation. Further, according to the committee, the differentiation of functions could be "spelled out" in two assumptions: (1) *"A sound program of teacher education preparation must provide* for [both] liberal and professional education." To achieve this, the teacher must have a liberal background comparable to a degree from a liberal arts college. Included in the liberal arts preparation, as prerequisite to professional study, should be the general foundation courses in the behavioral sciences and in history and philosophy of education. The specific academic emphasis—the teaching major and minor for secondary teachers, and a broader scholarly preparation for elementary teachers—should be completed in the undergraduate preparation. Professional preparation should represent fairly long periods of experience in public schools, and the student teachers should be supervised by cooperating teachers, carefully selected from the faculties of those schools; professional knowledge is best acquired through seminars specifically planned to integrate with the practical experience. (2) *"Programs for preparation of teachers* should be planned jointly by

---

7 The Sub-Committee (E. McCuistion, Chairman), *A Report on the Arkansas Experiment in Teacher Education,* The Experiment (September 1960).

faculties of education and liberal arts, each assuming primary re-sponsibility in their own areas."[8]

The committee, in defense of its postulates, noted that while neither of the assumptions by itself indicated a great departure from traditional practice, together they spelled a sharp break, since they met the two prerequisites for efficiency in teacher preparation: first, "the delineation of results expected from each segment of the program, and from each course within the segment"; and second, "the assignment and acceptance of responsibility for developing courses to achieve these results."

"Once these assumptions are accepted, teacher education becomes the responsibility of the entire faculty. At the same time, the liberal arts and professional segments are differentiated and autonomy for program building established."[9]

Although written originally and essentially for the Arkansas project, the foregoing statements (from President Jones' letter) and the rationale for the assumptions of the project capsulize the philosophical and structural core of the ten-year effort. A wide variety of attendant experiments and demonstrations in many institutions followed. In addition, many public schools were related to the projects in one way or another. Probably as much experimenting was done in teaching practices, the development of materials of instruction, and various techniques of presentation as was devoted to the actual preparation of the teachers.

Many years must pass before a correct assessment can be made of the net gains that have come to American education as a result of the activities of the Fund for the Advancement of Education. It is obviously debatable as to whether these activities actually produced a new trend in teacher education or only exploited and accelerated one that was already in existence. The latter contingency seems to be the better conclusion for the moment. Such a contention would be pointless, however, because ferment was produced where ferment was needed; impetus was provided whatever the intent of the impetus; and an issue was sharpened to a point which has caused many parties to re-examine their original prejudices and beliefs relative to the issue.

The total effect on programs of teacher education would appear

---

[8] *Ibid.*, pp. 3–4.
[9] *Ibid.*, p. 5.

to be the strengthening of both the academic background and the professional sequence. The basic format described in Chapter II has not been changed materially. General education, subject specialization, and professional sequence still remain. The area of practicum through the introduction of a paid internship has been substantially improved, since this practice allows a high degree of integration between theory and practice; but there is a real question as to the acceptance of the dichotomization principle. In fact, probably the opposite practice is developing—a merging of philosophy, a cooperative approach, and a disappearance of rigid lines between professional and academic points of view.

The Carnegie Corporation. Unlike the Fund for the Advancement of Education, the Carnegie Corporation approached the problems of teacher education from the standpoint of analysis and recommendation, rather than the infusion of vast sums of money into the operation of schools and training institutions. Over a long period, the Corporation has been interested in teacher welfare, and early in the twentieth century it created the Carnegie Foundation for the Advancement of Teaching. The more recent approach, however, has involved the subsidization of one of the nation's great scientists and retired university presidents. Dr. James Bryant Conant, in a series of studies of the American system of education, and the way teachers are prepared to conduct its complex of activities— instruction, administration, and counseling and guidance. The system's relationship to the public which sustains it is also studied.

Dr. Conant has revealed his analyses and certain broad conclusions in four publications.[10] It should be noted that Conant, admittedly, had no prior intimate knowledge of the schools and agencies he was to scrutinize. Hence, he and his staff rather thoroughly combed the literature pertaining to the units he proposed to study, and they made extensive visits to selected schools in order to see and analyze them firsthand.

Conant found the comprehensive nature of the secondary school system much to his liking, but he was disturbed at a number of its inadequacies, notably in the quantity and quality of the academic subjects. He was especially concerned at the lack of emphasis on,

---

[10] *The American High School Today, The Junior High School, Slums and Suburbs,* and *The Education of American Teachers.*

and special provision for, the academically talented and intellectually gifted students.

The final report, *The Education of American Teachers,* is a careful analysis not only of teacher education, but also of the total educational and cultural setting in which teacher education is carried on. Seventy-seven institutions were visited in 22 states. The wide variety in types of training institutions is reflected in the list. The educational systems of the 16 most populous states were analyzed. Interviews with individual teachers, administrators, professors, students, and laymen were conducted.

Conant frankly admitted that as a young professor of chemistry in his early teaching days, he shared the prejudice of his academic colleagues that college teachers who professed to teach others how to teach had no reason to exist at all at any level of the educational endeavor.[11] With equal candor he admitted that during his presidency of Harvard University, this attitude softened somewhat, and by the time he undertook the study of teacher education he recognized that the "what to teach *vs.* the how to teach" issue was the result of interacting forces and circumstances much deeper and more complex than an isolated intrafaculty squabble on a number of campuses.

During the study, this conviction was strengthened. Conant found much to criticize "on both sides of the fence."[12] Because of his academic background, he held a natural affinity with the world of the liberal arts and had a high respect for scholarly attainment. Hence, he started with the assumption that these are the very foundation stones of a quality teacher; yet he found a confused situation existing in the academic divisions of the colleges he studied. General education requirements varied widely. Freshman courses in English exhibited such variation as to indicate virtual anarchy in this area. Much the same diversity was found in mathematics, and a "confusing disparity" of offerings characterized the areas of social science, science, and the humanities. Moreover, although no generalizations were made about the quality of teaching in the academic areas, the implication was left that there is room for considerable improvement in this connection.

In the theory and practice of teaching, Conant identified four

---

[11] James B. Conant, *The Education of American Teachers* (New York: McGraw-Hill, Book Company, 1963), p. 1.
[12] *Ibid.,* p. 13.

components of the intellectual equipment that are prerequisite to the development of teaching skill: (1) the democratic social component (the development of attitudes toward social change which generally foster the survival of our free society); (2) an interest in the way behavior develops in groups of children (knowledge of the processes by which social behavior evolves); (3) a sympathetic knowledge of the growth of children; and (4) the principles of teaching. Components 3 and 4 evolve from the same stem—understanding the processes of individual motivation, and knowing the essential behavior of a teacher to bring maximum response from the learner.[13]

Conant rejected the premise that there is a science of education; he preferred to accept educational sciences or educational disciplines as the basic core of the professional sequence. These are the history, philosophy, sociology, and psychology of education. The professors who teach in these areas serve in the role of intermediaries between theory and practice, and, according to Conant, should not be professors of educational psychology, sociology, and so forth, but professors of the basic discipline involved, with a strong commitment to the public schools and their improvement.

Conant did not consider, at least in the report, two key questions that immediately arise. First, where should the intermediary professor be billeted? Should he stay in the college that houses the parent discipline (history, for example), or should he be a member of the faculty in an autonomous school or college of education? Second, the hierarchy systems of universities being what they are, *will* the intermediary professor make a strong commitment to public education? If he does, what happens to his status in the academic hierarchy?

Practice teaching was found by Conant to be the only essential course in the professional sequence for the training of teachers. This should be done under a functionary roughly comparable to the clinical professor in medicine, who is an outstanding practitioner in his field but who devotes a part of his talents to supervision of students in training. The educational equivalent presumably would be a master teacher still on the job most of the time, but who has in charge some student teachers assigned to his supervision.

---

[13] *Ibid.*, pp. 113*ff*.

Conant found a national body such as the National Council for Accreditation of Teacher Education—with considerable autonomy to determine whether a college may or may not be accredited to train teachers—to be out of harmony with the best interests of the public in obtaining quality teachers. There should be such a body, but it should be advisory only; and it should be on call by training institutions and by boards of education to make studies and recommendations relative to programs of preparation, employment policies, and the like.

The most controversial of all of the proposals in Conant's study (and the one that underscores the whole tone of the report) was the recommendation relative to certification requirements. For that reason, it is quoted below in its entirety:

> For certification purposes the state should require only (a) that a candidate hold a baccalaureate degree from a legitimate college or university, (b) that he submit evidence of having successfully performed as a student teacher under the direction of college and public school personnel in whom the State Department has confidence, and in a practice teaching situation of which the State Department approves, and (c) that he hold a specially endorsed teaching certificate from a college or university which in issuing the official document attests that the institution as a whole considers the person adequately prepared to teach in a designated field and grade level.[14]

If this pattern were to be followed, the training institution would certify that according to its best estimate (a consensus of the total institution: academic, professional, and administrative), student A is prepared to teach in discipline B or area C. The state, then, is held accountable to satisfy itself that this candidate can successfully do what the institution certifies he can do. This means that the state must develop some sort of criteria to determine "successful student teaching."

What specifically is done in preparing the student, and how consensus is reached as to his competency, both as a scholar and a student, are strictly internal matters within the confines of the institution. How the state develops its criteria is obviously its constitutional prerogative and legal responsibility. Clearly, Conant assumed that the nation can and will place great confidence in the integrity

---

[14] *Ibid.*, p. 210.

of the colleges and universities that train teachers. What is not so clear are his assumptions as to the stability of state departments of education, and of the legislatures that enact the basic laws under which the schools operate and teachers are certified.

Perhaps the genius of the Conant report is in its very ambiguity. If it is interpreted in one way, the school or college of education appears to be an anachronism and should be dispensed with. If it is read from the standpoint of another bias, the conclusion can be reached that an autonomous agency for teacher education within the university, is imperative, especially at the graduate level. The report can be shaded to mean that academia, in the broad sense of the term, has the greatest stake in the process; but from another angle, although academic proficiency is basic, the factors that count most in producing a finished teacher are professional and practical.

The people who have lived with the problems for many years would certainly agree with Dr. Conant that the forces, traditions, prejudices, and interrelationships involved in teacher education are deeper and more complex than they appear on casual examination. Satisfactory solutions will not come quickly or easily.

Activities within the Teaching Profession

The National Commission on Teacher Education and Professional Standards was established in 1946 by the National Education Association. It was charged with "carrying on a continuing program for the profession in matters of selection and recruitment, preparation, certification, inservice growth, and the advancement of professional standards, including standards for institutions that prepare teachers."[15]

The Commission, in an effort to discharge its responsibilities, called a number of conferences in order to seek direction and gather the ideas and concepts which practicing teachers at all levels felt were significant relative to teacher education. A special task force on New Horizons in Teacher Education and Professional Standards was created "to develop definitive statements . . . that would serve as guides for action at the local, state and national levels by TEPS

---

[15] The Task Force, *New Horizons for the Teaching Profession* (Washington, D.C.: The National Commission on Teacher Education and Professional Standards, NEA, 1961), p. vii.

and other professional organizations and individuals toward the complete professionalization of teaching."[16]

The Task Force made its report in 1961, and in 1963 the Commission published *a Position Paper on Teacher Education and Professional Standards,* which serves as a summary of its own work and which gives the report of the Task Force. This *Position Paper* is perhaps as true a reflection of the consensus of the practicing teaching profession as it is possible to develop. It is summarized here to indicate the concern of the profession for the education of its members. The authors set the stage in the introduction:

> A revolution of rising expectations characterizes American education today. Aroused by the need for improved educational opportunities for all, the teaching profession is striving to meet these expectations by getting the nation's schools and colleges staffed by none but excellent teachers and administrators. To this end, it searches for ways to attract and screen applicants for teacher education, improve the preparation and increase the competence of teachers, and protect the competent and eliminate the incompetent; and for favorable conditions of work, higher salaries, more authority for the profession in the handling of its own affairs, and greater public understanding and support.[17]

The Commission, like the Fund for the Advancement of Education, saw a revolution in progress, but not of the same type. Rather, it observed a cultural groundswell of rising expectation, but it did not identify any particular panacea to satisfy it. A searching, probing tension exists which has no real direction.

> In the search, confusion befogs both ends and means. Much advice and many slogans and panaceas are offered. The size and stubborn nature of social and educational problems lead some to despair and inaction, others to irritated and irrational action. Yet the need and the opportunity for constructive action remain.[18]

The constructive action has started and much has been done, but it is not yet time for either the nation or the profession to crystallize on any one approach, or blindly to follow any single channel to improvement.

---

[16] *Ibid.,* pp. viii–ix.

[17] National Commission on Teacher Education and Professional Standards, *a Position Paper* (Washington, D.C.: The National Education Association, 1963), p. 1.

[18] *Idem.*

The nation needs better schools and better teachers. There are no simple answers to the complex problems of producing such schools and teachers, but there are some directions that seem promising. The Commission notes the significant progress already made in improving the education of teachers and the standards of the profession but acknowledges that much remains to be done. No individual or group can claim omniscience in the matter of our concern, and progress depends largely upon the consolidation of interested forces. In the public interest, the profession itself should assume more responsibility for setting and enforcing standards of preparation and practice.[19]

The Commission in its *Position Paper* proposed that the advancements in teacher education, and the constant upgrading of professional standards, should proceed within a frame of reference that sets up certain guidelines, but that the process in a democratic society should always be one of constant evolution within the guidelines. There are premises, too, which indicate general direction without establishing a specific route.

Teaching is a profession only as its members qualify with the marks of professional persons; the marks indicate one who:

a. Is a liberally educated person.
b. Possesses a body of specialized skills and knowledges essential to the performance of his job.
c. Makes rational judgments and acts accordingly; accepts responsibility for the consequences of his judgments and actions.
d. Believes in his service to society.
e. Assumes responsibility with his colleagues in developing and enforcing standards and abides by these standards in his own practice.
f. Seeks new knowledge and skill in order to improve his practice.[20]

Education is a public responsibility, however, and the public in the discharge of this responsibility must decide the purposes of education and provide the resources, both moral and financial, to ensure effective progress in the enterprise.

Once the general goals have been established, *autonomy is requisite to professional effectiveness;* but it is achieved only as the public feels sufficient confidence in the profession to delegate some of its responsibility to it. The responsibility includes the obligation to design programs that will fulfill the established purposes, to establish

---

[19] *Ibid.,* p. 2.
[20] *Ibid.,* pp. 2*ff.*

standards and see that they are maintained in the preparation and practice of members of the profession, and to give the protection necessary for the security of members when they are engaged in the activities necessary in the discharge of their responsibility.

Many diverse groups must work together in education. Since the teaching profession requires many different types of preparation (having grown from different systems with different traditions), and since different functions and patterns of preparation for them are involved, "the essential unifying characteristics" should be sought and matured.

The differences must be recognized and respected; hence *the teaching profession must be open to diverse and conflicting opinion.* Critical analysis and free and responsible examination of different and contending points of view must be expected and welcomed.

High standards of preparation are essential for better education. Public confidence, adequate financial support, and—above all— the quality and quantity of teachers are almost entirely dependent on the level of admission standards to teacher education programs, and on the integrity and the level of the programs in producing highly educated teachers qualified to carry out their responsibilities.

Innovation is essential to progress in teacher education. The best in tradition should be respected and kept, but new approaches, bold experimentation, and creativity are necessary to meet the challenges of an increasingly mobile and burgeoning population, the development of knowledge, the application of new technology to educational problems, and the perplexing international developments.

Based on the foregoing premises, the Commission divided its recommendations into six categories; selection, preparation, continuing education, regulation of standards, theory, and research. The recommendations are much too lengthy to be abstracted here; but, in summary, the TEPS Commission called for the selection of an adequate number of students to enter the teaching profession. These students should meet high admission standards, based on such factors as intelligence, academic achievement, physical stamina and health, emotional stability, and moral and ethical fitness. The faculties of the training institutions must be responsible for adopting the standards, but they should be adopted only after consultation with practicing teachers, school administrators, and state departments of education. In order to check the adequacy of the standards, a system of personnel services and follow-up studies should be established for constant checking of students after they have graduated and accepted teaching positions.

The most important element in teacher education programs is the competence of the faculties that conduct them. From the axiom that teachers will teach much as they have been taught and inspired, the conclusion is reached that college teachers should be "exceptional human beings—sensitive, curious, creative, intelligent, and ethical." Although this pertains particularly to the education faculty, teacher education is an "across the board" responsibility of the total faculty, and the student in training should be the recipient of master teaching in all his classes while in college. The Commission stressed balance in the curriculum between general education, subject-matter specialization, and professional courses and student teaching, with roughly 80 per cent of the time devoted to the general education and academic preparation. In addition, sizable blocks of time should be devoted to field experience. Four years are not enough for these activities; a period of five years is necessary to complete even the minimal experience and academic pattern. A paid internship jointly supervised by the schools and colleges ideally should follow the five-year preservice program and should be in addition to the student teaching experience.

The Commission would make the colleges basically responsible for planning, conducting, and evaluating their programs; but the final test is always the performance of the graduate subsequent to his preservice education. Here the local teachers association, boards of education, and laymen generally have a responsibility to provide an environment conducive to continuing development.

The Commission recommended that a nonpolitical, but legally recognized, board or commission or council be established in each state; such a board should be broadly representative of the teaching profession at all levels. This agency should have advisory responsibility for (1) the development of policy and requirements for the accreditation of teacher education institutions; (2) the issuance and revocation of licenses; and (3) continuing study to design better procedure for improving standards of licensure, accreditation, and assignment. The Commission further recommended that the National Council for the Accreditation of Teacher Education be maintained as an autonomous agency, free from pressure or dictation by its constituent groups, but always sensitive to their recommendations. The NCATE should be broadly representative of the teaching profession at all levels (elementary, secondary, and college), and it should continue to examine the total teacher education program—academic and professional—in each institution it accredits.

Finally, the Commission stressed the development of theory and research as basic to improvement in teacher education. A broad roster of activity is indicated here: descriptive studies, demonstration, experimentation, and sophisticated analysis of learning theory and its application to practice. Most important, however, are the studies and research which "sharply define teaching excellence and the discrete body of knowledge that is foundational in the professional preparation of teachers."

CHAPTER VI

The Teacher of the Future— A Projection

Two traditions have been competitive in the evolution of teacher education in the United States. One has its roots in the combination of forces that shaped the national character and produced a unique system of public education. The other, for want of a definitive name, may be termed academia, altered somewhat by its modern trappings, but, still, clearly the offspring of its classical beginnings.

Teacher education began as a byproduct of the growing literacy needs of a young republic, sure of its destiny but unwilling to chart a long-term course to achieve it. So the whole nineteenth century, and the early decades of the twentieth, educationally were "played by ear." The federal constitution granted the control of education to the states; the states, in turn, ostensibly delegated (but in reality defaulted) their constitutional responsibility to local districts; and the districts did the best they could under the circumstances, which in too many instances was not very much. Strangely, however, out of this extremely loose and uncoordinated procedure, some remarkably firm cultural commitments emerged. The schools would be free—that is, free of tuition; they would be compulsory, universal, and secular; and although the concept was never expressed in concrete terms, they would remain extraordinarily sensitive to that segment of the society which supported them.

Universal schools, in the formative years of the nation, meant elementary schools—places where children could learn to read, write, and do numbers. There was nothing particularly intellectual or mystical about the business. It was a pragmatic process, mainly a routine job of disciplinary control of the youngsters while they were drilled in the fundamentals. Someone, however, had to be in charge: a teacher. This person did not need to be highly educated or especially competent from an intellectual standpoint. The exigencies of the situation demanded a certain toughness and some elementary knowledge and skills, but nothing out of the ordinary.

For this type of teacher, operating in the relatively unsophisticated cultural environment of the times, a simple, direct, and inexpensive training program seemed to be indicated. The normal schools provided the answer. Teachers in considerable numbers were needed, and they were provided. The success of the normal schools was quantitative. No one who has studied the early development of these schools would claim any degree of intellectual quality for either their program or their product. Since they were spawned by an embryo educational system that was charting its route as it moved along, the normal schools naturally adopted the custom of very close liaison with the immediate regions and school systems they served. As a result, the value structure of professional education has remained closely attuned to the ebb and flow of social emphasis as it has been reflected in the public school system.

A New Base is Necessary

A cultural frame of reference for teacher education ("grass roots" oriented and originally custom-tooled to fit the needs of a raw frontier society) has developed in the United States; but along with it has been the resurgence of the classical, scholarly tradition in American colleges and universities, and—to a lesser extent—in some of the secondary schools. This tradition has consistently held that knowledge, scholarship, and true intellectual development transcend national and cultural boundaries, and should not be conditioned by the provincial needs of any region or state. Since teaching should be concerned chiefly with developing the intellect, the training pattern for teachers should be similarly concerned with the development of superior intellectual qualities in the potential teacher.

Merging traditions. To a certain extent the traditions have merged. At least a working compromise has been achieved. Whether it is genuine or only a temporary plateau in a long-term struggle remains to be seen. One conclusion, however, is clear: The nation cannot long afford the luxury of an educational contest where neither contender will yield the historical base of his position. A new platform is needed where the best of both traditions can be melded into a single approach to the problems involved in teacher education.

Obsolescence in present practice.   The foundations for the development of such a base already are apparent. Teachers educated today—no matter what balance has been achieved between the academic and professional segments of the program—are prepared to serve in an obsolete role and to teach in an obsolete way. This is not because their training institutions have failed them or because there is friction within the ranks of teacher educators. The difficulty is much broader than the shortcomings of any training pattern.

The Imbalance in Modern Society

Actually, the problem is an imbalance that has developed in the total complex of human society. One narrow channel of man's enterprise has outdistanced all the others. Research, especially in the physical and biological sciences and in engineering, has created some breakthroughs and some attendant achievements that the rest of the structure simply has not been able to absorb. Orbital flight is perhaps only the most dramatic of these. The social, political, and economic systems of the earth have not kept pace; hence the whole structure is out of equilibrium.

The historical pattern would indicate that now these interlocking systems would go through a long and painful period of adjustment lasting a century or more, but that luxury is no longer available. Mankind is faced with a harsh dilemma. Man must learn to adjust quickly, intelligently, and according to a rational pattern, or he must face the complete dislocation of his society.

The place of education.   The key to the dilemma is education. If the coming generations can be educated properly, they have a chance to meet the challenge successfully. Education is a process concerned with changes in the individual and collective behavior of the human family. Such changes are directly related to what people learn, to how they learn it, and to what end they apply it.

Forces Shaping Tomorrow's World

All who are currently interested in teacher education need to ask some searching questions. They should seek a fresh approach to the preparation of personnel— an approach that will stimulate the kind of learning tomorrow's world will require. Before this can be done, however, something of the dimensions of that world must be discovered. What combination of forces and circumstances and phenomena are to be dealt with?

No one would deny that the circumstances are complex, the forces potent, and some of the phenomena beyond human powers of conception; but now the pattern of the national existence is being redirected in ways that are not clearly comprehended. Somehow, leaders must find ways to cope with a world population that will double each half-century unless it can be controlled. An educational system must be devised to incorporate the new knowledge that is being produced by research and scientific inquiry into the curriculums of the schools. Agencies must be provided to spread both old and new knowledge over more and more of the earth's population. Learning must somehow be adjusted to accommodate the needs of the underdeveloped sections of the world, as well as those of the more intellectually sophisticated areas.

New and troublesome problems will arise between the so-called "have" and "have not" peoples. The current struggle between two great power systems—the Western nations led by the United States, and the coalition of communist countries headed by the Soviet Union, could quickly erupt into a cataclysmic war. Apparently, however, this contest may stop short of military strife and evolve into a total, comprehensive, but none the less brutal competition for possession of the world's economic, physical, intellectual, and spiritual resources. The struggle seems to demand that the entire cultural complex of both opponents be committed in a no-quarter-asked-or-given battle, which has overtones that can be neither softened nor silenced by any tried and true formula out of past experience. Man's future appears to depend upon the level of his imagination and creativeness, and upon the amount of innovation and originality he can command in inventing new formulas to serve his needs. In short, can he design new educative processes, develop and implement more precise learning techniques, and produce more sophisticated, intellectual responses across the broad spectrum of human ability before it is too late?

The Foundations of Current Practice
in Teacher Education

The teacher who has been educated in a modern college or university is not equipped for long to keep abreast of today's fast-moving forces. The main reason for this situation probably lies in the fact that, in general, the academic climate in the United States is oriented to the past rather than to the future, and the departments and schools and colleges of education are no exception. As has been noted repeatedly, teacher education is a division of the collegiate enterprise that has deep roots in the past, and its history goes back to the very beginnings of formal education. Teacher education entered the modern scene by way of the normal school movement of the nineteenth century, and herein lies at least a part of the problem. A procedure has been developed which philosophically is part classical, part Rousseau, part Pestalozzi, and part Dewey, among others; and the pattern has retained some of the normal-school influence along with a modern touch that research has indicated. This complex also contains a varied assortment of folklore that goes all the way back to the time of Socrates.

A teacher model, a teaching process, and a deep educational tradition has emerged from this procedure. They have served with reasonable credit in the past, but it is now time to examine the model and the process as well as the tradition. A new model is needed to satisfy the exigencies of the future.

The Current Teacher Model

To prepare a teacher in the past design, a remarkably standardized procedure has been developed. With local variations, the same pattern is found in almost every training institution. An attempt is made to start with a reasonably mature personality as the basic foundation. Upon this an attempt is made to develop a block of fairly sophisticated intellectual attainment in one or more of the scholarly disciplines. Some facility in teaching design and communication is added to the framework, along with an attempt to teach the rudimentary skills of counseling and guidance. Since most of the states have legally placed the school and/or the teacher *in loco parentis,* this is interpreted to mean that the candidate must be equipped to contribute to the learner's moral and spiritual values, to his development as a citizen, and to his ability to live comfortably with the manners, mores, and customs of his society. Finally, miscellaneous assignments are included, ranging from the creation of instructional materials to serving as a public relations agent in explaining the purposes and needs of education.

Briefly outlined, this is the structure that has been fabricated as a training program, and the program produces a package containing personality, intellect, skills, and competencies in varying degrees of excellence—a teacher. The term "package" is not intended to be trite, because this is exactly what the training program has set out to produce. It has attempted to develop in one functionary a comprehensive ability to take a young learner at a given point for a given purpose and remain virtually self-contained throughout the entire process.

Teacher performance vs. quality of learning. A careful analysis of the program in modern teacher education leads to the conviction that a premium has been placed on one talent above all others: the art of *adlibitum,* or "adlibbing" as it has come to be known. It denotes the ability to conduct a process with which one is most familiar, but which is never quite the same from one performance to another. It is a combination of word fluency and sharp intellectual response, always within a familiar setting and with familiar material, but where the performer departs from the script with impunity or extemporizes as he goes along. This is an ability of high order, and there is a tendency to make it synonymous with great teaching. Certainly, no one would deny that it is at least one of the ingredients of a master performance, for without it a teacher would be dull and colorless.

It is possible, however, that a pattern has evolved which, perhaps inadvertently, stresses teacher performance more than the learning process. While a masterful teacher performance is a significant part of any learning situation, the major emphasis must always be concerned with the impact of that performance on the growth of the learner. In setting up a proposed model as a target for future programs in teacher education, this factor will be in the background as one of the primary concerns.

A Proposed Teacher Model

The teacher is still at the center of the process, but the function is changed, and the relationship to the dynamic is altered. He may be likened to a master of ceremonies or to the producer, rather than to the main actor. He is equipped with the ability to use effectively the techniques and devices that are available, and his responsibility is to focus these—along with his own talents—on a given learning situation. Graphically, the design would place the teacher in position as a sort of central sun, which controls certain satellite processes.

Five such satellites may be suggested here: (1) *the teaching media,* including television, films, radio, projection devices, and various types of audio equipment; (2) *the teaching team,* which presupposes breaking the teaching act into related but specialized functions, such as design, communication, research, and presentation; (3) *programmed teaching devices* for individualized learning and immediate reinforcement of learner responses; (4) *the teaching system,* which is a preplanned and articulated design for teaching an entire discipline from its elementary beginnings to the point where the learner is self-sufficient; (5) *the research complex* that is building up around learning theory, teaching technique, and learner growth.

Competencies for the Future Model

The teacher who can know, live with, and effectively use this constellation of devices, techniques, ideas, and concepts obviously must be a superior person. It is a sobering prospect to contemplate the program of education necessary to produce such a functionary. From the outset, it should be made perfectly clear that the professional competencies must be built upon a solid foundation of knowledge and a tough scholarly acumen that leaves no doubt as to the superior intellectual qualities of the person involved. Beyond this base of knowledge and a highly developed intellectual capacity, three major interlocking competencies will be necessary: the ability to achieve synthesis, the ability to execute coordination, and the ability to serve in a catalyst role.

The ability to achieve synthesis. Synthesis is putting together a combination of separate parts into a balanced whole. In this case, it would be an enterprise where the learner component is the focus of a complex of many elements. He is placed in a learning situation designed to help him get something—a unit of knowledge, an attitude, or a skill—or to help him change in some way or to adjust to some situation. The material, skill, or attitude to be learned is broken down into teachable units. A teaching design is fashioned for each one. An approach is determined. Aids and devices are selected and arranged into the proper sequence. These are only illustrative of the many elements involved. One could include the apperception level of the learner, the tempo that fits his maturation rate. If more than one learner is included, the situation is further complicated by decisions as to what should be group process, what should be individualized, and so on. A skilled synthesist would first visualize the separate elements, then formulate them into a pattern, and finally develop a plan of execution.

The ability to coordinate. Coordination is closely related to the ability of synthesis. Where synthesis means visualizing, planning, and putting together a balanced operation, coordination means the maintenance of general harmony within the going enterprise. Here the concern is with timing, tone, temperament, and the smooth functioning of each part in relation to the other parts.

The ability to serve as a catalyst. In the role of catalyst the teacher plays a solo part. In many ways this is the premier performance. It is essentially what a teacher exists for. Synthesis has been achieved; the operation has been coordinated; now the teacher turns his total effort to what is happening as a result of the operation. The learner is the focus of his entire attention. The gadgets, devices, and techniques are incidental now. What the learner is getting, how it is coming through to him, how he is managing it, what it is doing to him, and what he proposes to do with it are the major concerns. Learning becomes the great drama; learner growth, the great achievement. At times the teacher may wish to insert himself into the operation to speed up or slow down the reaction, or he may wish to remain relatively detached to observe, to contemplate, or to project results into future plans.

The Education of the Future Model

To this point the act of teaching has been viewed as it presently is done, and a different model has been proposed as a possible answer to the demanding specifications of the future. The next logical question concerns the type of preparation program that would produce the quality of teacher performance indicated.

The process of selection. The major question is selection. Is the aim to prepare a functionary that can be produced, or to find one born with just the right combination of chromosones that, whatever the training pattern, will develop into a teaching genius? The answer to the question for the moment must be assumed. First, high-quality human material is essential. Part of the components involved are certainly innate, but beyond this base the educational pattern, both in structured experiences and formal schooling, will be crucial.

The factors that should be looked for in the selection of candidates will be a task for the research people. To date, no satisfactory indexes have been developed. Certainly, however, a high degree of sensitivity is called for, plus a promise of creative talent and innovativeness, and above all some indication of dedication to the human family and its problems. Teacher-trainers will need to know if they can find these ingredients ready-made, or if they can be developed, or if they must look for a certain base potential and build on it. Further, is the sought-for goal an experience pattern, a specific home background, the opportunity for free inquiry throughout the growth cycle, a life of hardship and travail, a carefree life, or perhaps a combination of all of these?

The formal training program. Any attempt to list specifics at this point would be foolhardy. This will be a long-term process, but certainly the future will witness a long overdue phenomenon. The traditional pattern will be redesigned according to the goals that are sought. The aim will be to develop a person possessing a rich store of knowledge concerning the heritage of his civilization. He should be specialized in some branch of it, and he should be intellectually acute and independent in scholarship. To achieve such objectives implies a commitment from more than the staff of the college of education. It implies channels that cut across college and departmental lines, and it implies that the disciplines have a responsibility at least as important as research and the development of research specialists of high quality.

Through a careful blending of campus and field experiences, the line that divides theory from practicum should be erased as nearly as possible. The activities involved in this procedure must be worked out for each candidate individually, but all students will spend much time in different types of communities observing the phenomena they have studied formally in school. They will see how a community operates. The concept of power and its application in the political mechanisms of communities, states, and the nation will become part of their working knowledge, because they will have seen the real thing and know how it functions. They will observe education as a social enterprise in the culture. They will know its evolution, study its problems, learn firsthand the conflicting philosophies that keep it in turmoil, and see the progress that has been made despite the turmoil.

The teacher of tomorrow will learn in his preparation program that a community has competing values within its organisms. He will know that he must contend with value conflicts, because he will have seen how they affect the citizens of the community. He will see that each youngster has developed his own private radar for sensing what the community thinks is important; the teacher will see how each one shapes his life objectives in conformity or in conflict with the community's value structure.

The fledgling teacher will note that some of the youngsters do not make an adequate adjustment. He will see the result in the adult misfits and castoffs. He will observe the erosion of emotional conflict, the result of tragedy, the impact of accident.

If this series of controlled experiences is incorporated properly into the training pattern, each teacher should approach his task with the definite understanding that people are his forte, the community his shop, and knowledge and wisdom his tools.

Bibliography

Adams, James Truslow, *The Epic of America*. Boston: Little, Brown & Company, 1952.

Alexander, William M., and Galen Saylor, *Modern Secondary Education*. New York: Holt, Rinehart & Winston, Inc., 1959.

The American Association of Teachers Colleges, Yearbooks Sixth through Twenty-Sixth, The Association, Oneonta, N.Y.

Armstrong, W. E. and T. M. Stinnett, *A Manual on Certification Requirements for School Personnel in the United States*. Washington, D.C.: National Commission on Teacher Education and Professional Standards, National Education Association, 1957.

Beck, R. H., Walter W. Cook, and Nolan C. Kearney, *Curriculum in the Elementary School*, 2nd ed. Englewood Cliffs, N.J.: Prentice-Hall, Inc., 1960.

Butts, R. Freeman, *A Cultural History of Education*. New York: McGraw-Hill Book Company, 1947.

Conant, James Bryant, *The Education of American Teachers*. New York: McGraw-Hill Book Company, 1963.

Cottrell, Donald P., ed., *Teacher Education for a Free People*. Oneonta, N.Y.: The American Association of Colleges for Teacher Education, 1956.

Cubberley, E. P., *The Certification of Teachers*, Fifth Yearbook, National Society for the Scientific Study of Education. Chicago: University of Chicago Press, 1906.

Davis, Calvin Olin, *A History of the North Central Association of Colleges and Secondary Schools, 1895–1945*. Ann Arbor, Mich.: The Association, 1945.

Geise, John, *Man and the Western World*. New York: Harcourt, Brace & World, Inc., 1940.

Mulhern, James, *A History of Education*, 2nd ed. New York: The Ronald Press Company, 1959.

Pangburn, Jessie M., *The Evolution of the American Teachers College*. New York: Teachers College, Columbia University Contributions to Education, No. 500, Bureau of Publications, 1932.

The Professional Standards Movement in Teaching: Progress and Projection, Report of the Parkland, Washington, Conference. Washington, D.C.: National Commission on Teacher Education and Professional Standards, National Education Association, 1956.

A Report on the Arkansas Experiment in Teacher Education. New York: The Fund for the Advancement of Education, Ford Foundation, 1960.

Van Til, William, Gordon F. Vars, and John H. Lounsbury, *Modern Education for the Junior High School Years*. Indianapolis: Bobbs-Merrill Company, Inc. 1961.

Woodring, Paul, *New Directions in Teacher Education*. New York: The Fund for the Advancement of Education, Ford Foundation, 1957.

Index